PSYCHOTHERAPISTS AS EXPERT WITNESSES

DATE DUE

PSYCHOTHERAPISTS AS EXPERT WITNESSES

Families at Breaking Point

Roger Kennedy

KARNAC

LONDON   NEW YORK

First published in 2005 by
H. Karnac (Books) Ltd.
6 Pembroke Buildings, London NW10 6RE

British Library Cataloguing in Publication Data

A C.I.P. for this book is available from the British Library

ISBN 1 85575 372 3

Edited, designed and produced by The Studio Publishing Services Ltd, Exeter EX4 8JN

Printed in Great Britain by Hobbs the Printers Ltd, Totton, Hampshire

10 9 8 7 6 5 4 3 2 1

www.karnacbooks.com

CONTENTS

ABOUT THE AUTHOR

Roger Kennedy was trained in child psychiatry at the Tavistock Centre and at Guy's Hospital. He has been Consultant Psychotherapist, Family Service, Cassel Hospital since 1982, and he is an Honorary Senior Lecturer in Psychiatry at Imperial College London. He is a training analyst, President Elect, British Psychoanalytical Society, and the author of many papers and several books.

CHAPTER ONE

Introduction—the expert and the courts

What is an expert?

Being a so-called "expert witness" in Family Law carries with it an awesome responsibility; recommendations made by the expert may well help to determine the future life of a child and their family. As Mr Justice Wall (2002, p. 76) helpfully defined it, the term expert refers to persons who are external to the court proceedings and whom the court invites in, to enable them to advise on specific issues relating to the interests of the child. As he put it, appropriate expert evidence about what should happen to a child can be of crucial importance in guiding the court's decision about what is in the child's best interests, although this should be needed only in the more complex or contentious cases.

Courts generally welcome the help that they receive from good and unbiased expert evidence, though the judge has to make the final decision in the case. The aim of this book is to describe, with detailed and disguised case studies, some of the author's experiences from the last twenty years of assessing difficult family situations. There will be a mixture of general points about the role of the expert and specific details from individual case studies in order to illustrate issues. While the focus will be on the role of the psychiatrist as expert, many of the points made could be applied to expert evidence given by other professionals, such as psychologists and psychotherapists.

Although I work as a child and adult psychiatrist, my training and experience as a psychoanalyst complements my approach to this kind of work. Psychoanalysis can be seen fundamentally as a body of theoretical and clinical knowledge concerned with looking at people's conflicts, feelings, anxieties, and reasons for action, which includes an understanding of the unconscious processes of the mind. I see my work as involving an applied psychoanalytic approach that is using psychoanalysis to understand the nature of the process involved with individuals, their relationships to each other and within a family context, as well as their interactions with the legal structures. This approach will, I hope, become clear through the many clinical examples given in the text. It involves making contact with people in difficult circumstances; it requires patient and highly skilled listening, attention to anxieties, defences, the subtleties of personality, as well as an openness to the unknown.

Quite often, the analyst has to face calmly and thoughtfully very disturbing feelings emanating from patients, a skill that I would suggest is indispensable when undertaking an assessment of a disturbed family. The ability to withstand the impact of powerful and conflicting emotions is also very helpful when dealing with many disturbed families over several years. This is a field where professionals easily "burn out", because they cannot deal with the emotional impact of their work. A psychoanalytical approach based upon the need of the professional to "metabolize" their reactions to being in the firing line with their clients is essential. The analytic view respects the complexities and subtleties of the human mind, seeing the mind as multi-layered and full of depth; as such it can be helpful in counterbalancing the more crisis-led approach to child care issues, where decisions have to be made, and made at times with speed.

There will be an attempt to go through in detail the various elements of the expert assessment, in order to provide a clear and comprehensive guide to workers in the field. In addition, there will be various comments on how the system actually works, *warts and all*, as well as some suggestions on how to deal with difficulties, in order to give a realistic picture of what happens when professionals are involved in the court proceedings.

The case studies will use material from both Public Law and Private Law. Public Law cases refer to those where a local authority seeks a care or supervision order; the families in these circumstances are usually highly disordered and displaying many problems, with the children often potentially at risk from various kinds of child abuse. The questions asked of the expert will often include an opinion about whether or not a child should remain with their parents. Private Law cases are usually disputes between parents or other family members over residence or contact, where, for example, one parent may have been violent or has had emotional or psychiatric problems.

Sometimes a psychiatrist may be asked by a local authority to make an assessment of a family without court involvement, but issues arising from that assessment may lead the professionals to turn to the court for judgement; for example, if child abuse is detected and decisions need to be made about a child's future. The psychiatrist may then have to reorientate their opinions around the court structure, taking account of the need to write a court report, and to attend the court where their views will be put to the test. This can be a daunting prospect for even the most experienced practitioner. Lawyers are expert in looking at the meaning of words; they will look at every phrase that the expert has used, every shade of meaning that can be teased out of the report, whether or not the expert had been aware of all the implications of their recommendations. It can be exhausting being cross-examined, sometimes for several hours at a stretch; the expert has to deal with a language and a process that may bear little resemblance to their own training. It is hoped that this book will provide some guidance for the anxious mental health professional in their hour of need, as well as for lawyers wishing to use expert evidence to help clarify issues around children and families.

In this chapter, I discuss a number of general points concerned with how the courts deal with experts, and experts with courts, as well as looking at the nature of expert evidence.

Chapter Two discusses in detail the assessment of families, as a backdrop to the rest of the book, which will describe a selection of different family situations that needed a court report.

Chapter Three gives three clinical examples from my own practice of how one has to deal with the "best worst option" in many family cases.

Chapter Four considers residence and contact issues through a number of clinical examples, including families where there has been domestic violence.

Chapter Five looks at issues concerning whether or not a family should be rehabilitated, following removal of children. This will also cover some issues concerning adoption and fostering, and will include examples from multi-disciplinary work.

Chapter Six presents a summary of issues, and concludes with ideas about how the law could be changed to become more child focused, based on issues brought up throughout the book.

No perfect solutions

From a number of perspectives the work described in these chapters is not easy. It can take considerable time to read through documentation, to see the family members, to write a report and, if necessary, to appear in court, though it is not always necessary for the expert to appear. Sometimes what has been written is enough to help resolve a situation, if all parties are in agreement with the views expressed. When the parties cannot resolve a conflict, or when there is a disagreement about recommendations, then an expert may well be called to give evidence, but they may also appear in complex situations that require a good deal of discussion to resolve, either just before going into court or in meetings some time beforehand. Then it may happen that it is only after examination that the expert's views become clear, particularly if new evidence comes to light, or old evidence is put forward by counsel in a new way. At such times the court process can be more like a fruitful dialogue than a battleground.

It can be emotionally taxing to face the family's fears, hopes, anxieties, and problems, while trying to remain as independent as possible. It can also be very stressful appearing in court, where one's clinical judgement may be examined in minute detail and where one's views must be presented in plain language, although it can be a stimulating challenge to have to justify views in open court, and will certainly deeply affect how one puts together clini-cal arguments. It can still be emotionally draining to sit through sometimes hours of cross-examination, even with a judge who does his or her best to protect the expert from the enthusiastic interven-tions from barristers. For the beginner reading this text, it is perhaps useful to know that even the most experienced profes-sional can occasionally come away from court feeling battered and bruised. It can be tempting to deal with the strain of such work by siding with the family or, indeed, with the other professionals involved, rather than maintain a neutral position, regardless of who has initiated the request for the opinion.

But it is perhaps the responsibility itself that is most taxing for the expert, because the direction of a child's future life may hang in the balance. While the decisions involved in these situations may not be as acutely dramatic as those involved in saving a child's life in an operating theatre or on a paediatric ward, they are none the less as potentially crucial for the child's future, determining, for example, whether or not they are to remain with the parents, or to have increased contact with an absent parent; whether or not broth-ers and sisters may have to be split up, or a parent removed from the family home in order to give the other parent a chance to keep their children. Issues about fostering, adoption, contact, whether or not a child and their parents need treatment, and, if so, what kind, are frequent issues to be faced.

The majority of judges are aware of the complexities of these situations, and convey a willingness to listen carefully to the evi-dence and keep an open mind about what should happen. Time and again one is reminded of Solomon's judgement about the two "har-lots" living in the same house, who came to him with a claim about each being the mother of one baby (1 Kings 3, 16–28). One of the babies had died and the mother then stole the other woman's live baby. As is well known, Solomon threatened to divide the living baby in two with his sword and give each woman half. The real mother would rather the other woman have the baby than this hap-pen to her child. In a sense, the sort of issues dealt with in the family court are not that dissimilar, in that a judgement has to be made about who has the child's true welfare at heart. While the physical division of the child is not an issue, one is certainly often faced with how children feel psychologically divided by parental attitudes.

The courts usually do what they can to make the children's lives more satisfactory, but this is a field where choosing the "best worst" option is often all that can be managed. There are no ideal solutions; the children are faced with suffering whatever is decided. It can be beneficial for the children to give them the chance, if they wish, to receive some focal psychotherapeutic work to help them give voice to their feelings of frustration and uncertainty. It is also asserted by some professionals that one should only work with the children when their future is certain. This, however, means that they would then receive little or no help for months on end, by which time they may be so traumatized that effective work with them is too late.

When to use an expert

An expert is not needed for every difficult family case. As Mr Justice Wall stated, "the Court should give permission to instruct outside expert evidence only if that evidence is relevant to a particular issue in the case and necessary for the proper disposal of the case" (Wall, 2002, p. 79). Often local professionals can deal with a complex family problem, and they have the advantage of knowing the family over the course of time. An *outside expert* can be useful in the following circumstances:

- When the outside expert has a particular expertise that needs to be called upon, such as a specialized paediatric opinion about a child's injuries, or when there is an issue about whether or not a family should undergo intensive rehabilitation.
- When a neutral view of the whole situation is requested by one or more parties, perhaps because the family and their local workers have become locked in unsatisfactory ways of relating to one another.
- When local professionals feel their own therapeutic work may become compromised by being too involved with the court process.
- When local professionals do not have the time, willingness, expertise, or resources to go through the lengthy process of a court assessment.

Occasionally the only motivation for having an expert comes from one party, such as the Children's Guardian, or a parent's lawyer, but they do have to persuade others, and ultimately a judge, to allow an independent expert to be instructed. Usually the various workers who know the family are only too happy to have a new view of a situation, and, indeed, may actively commission the expert, but there are occasions when local professionals feel put out by someone coming from the outside to view their work. The expert then needs to be rather tactful in engaging with the local workers. At the same time, the local workers need to feel less territorial in their attitudes.

Different courts

For those unfamiliar with family court proceedings, these may take place at various levels: at a Magistrate's Court, the County Court, the Principal Registry in High Holborn, and in the High Court, either in London or outside London on a "circuit" where a High Court Judge is sitting. Generally, the more complex cases are heard in the higher courts. Occasionally, the Court of Appeal may become involved in a decision about a family, as will be described in a later chapter (p. 00). The House of Lords has also occasionally become involved in clarifying the interpretation of Family Law. Indeed, it made a landmark ruling in 1997 that has greatly influenced the degree to which judges can influence the assessment of facilities. As a result of its judgement *Re C (Interim Care Order: Residential Assessment) (1997) AC 489,* judges have been given the power to order a local authority to fund a family assessment under Section 38(6) of the Children Act 1989. This has meant that many families who would not have had a chance of assessment by an expert of one sort or another, have been allowed access to expert opinion.

For some time, judges were deemed to be able only to order assessments and not treatments, as a result of another subsequent judgement in the High Court on a Cassel Hospital family—*Re: M (Residential Assessment Directions)* [1998] 2 FLR 371. However, this judgement has now been superseded by *Re G* [2004] EWCA Civ 24, where the Court of Appeal looked at evidence from another Cassel family. The latter recent landmark decision has eliminated the distinction between assessment and treatment, and has brought into sharp focus the importance of incorporating the European Human Rights legislation in this sort of work. This new judgement goes back to *Re C* and judges that it is important to retain a broad concept of assessment in these difficult cases, one that may well include various kinds of treatment. The judges also point out that the costs of extensive litigation in these cases could be used to fund a family admission.

The role of the psychiatrist

The work referred to in this book mainly concerns that of the psychiatrist; specifically that of the child psychiatrist, but also occasionally that of the adult psychiatrist. Psychiatrists are trained first as doctors and then specialize in general psychiatry before, if they wish, specializing in a sub speciality such as child psychiatry. The work of the adult psychiatrist is mainly concerned with seriously ill mental patients, such as those suffering from schizophrenia, bipolar disorders, and severe depression. Patients with anorexia nervosa, learning disabilities, or drug abuse may be seen by more specialized psychiatrists. Forensic adult psychiatrists will be concerned with those suffering from mental illness and severe personality disorders who have been involved with the criminal law. There is a substantial body of patients who end up seeing a psychiatrist because of various kinds of personality difficulties that may involve them self-harming, feeling suicidal, and having difficulty sustaining relationships. Such patients often do not respond to psychotropic drug therapy and resources for them have been patchy. Adult psychiatrists often do not feel they have the resources to treat them, and yet these patients may end up in mental hospital beds or draining the emotional and financial resources of local services. Consultant medical psychotherapists, who have training first as general psychiatrists and then specialize in various kinds of psychotherapy, are specifically trained to deal with such patients, though there are not many such consultant posts in existence at the moment, particularly outside London. However, the government have recently targeted personality disorder patients as a priority, and local services are being encouraged by various means to set up appropriate services for them. A number of the adults in those families who come into contact with the courts have a personality disorder, and hence the psychiatrist has a role in their assessment. The psychoanalyst, and the psychoanalytically informed psychiatrist, also have an important role here as they have extensive experience or working with patients with personality disorders.

Lord Justice Thorpe has addressed the issue of how the assessment of personality contributes to decisions in family law in two landmark papers. In the first paper (1993), he raises the theme as important because in issues of child care and protection the assessment of the capacity to parent is crucial to the placement decision, and such an assessment requires a survey of the attributes and qualities that form part of the general character or personality of the parents. Personality refers to the "enduring and predictable qualities or characteristics which determine the individual's behaviour in diverse circumstances" (Thorpe, 1993, p. 294).

In his second paper, Thorpe (1994) sounds a note of caution about the fallibility of human judgement when the court comes to making decisions about child care matters, including that of personality assessment. Safeguards against human error include accumulated professional experience, self-knowledge, and detachment. He concludes by observing that the task of assessing personality is formidably difficult, particularly as human beings can be strongly and expertly defended, and their social presentation may be assured and convincing while they may be hiding what they really feel. For this reason, one could add that a psychiatrist with psychotherapeutic skills can have a particularly useful role in assessing parents' personalities, as they are used to dealing with resistant patients and are also experienced in assessing and treating those with personality problems.

In assessing personality, one looks at the history, the development of the individual, the nature of their past and present relationships, and the relation of past experiences to current behaviour. Sometimes separate psychological testing by a psychologist may be helpful, for example if there is an element of learning disability. Overall, the interviewing psychiatrist is looking for any patterns in the way that the individual organizes their behaviour, beliefs, motivatations, and values. Patterns of self/other interactions are particularly crucial in forming judgements about the nature of the personality, as well as specific items of history such as past depression or suicidal behaviour. A difficult but important aspect of the clinical judgement of personality concerns the degree to which there is a sense of integration, the person's sense of their own identity, or, on the contrary, a lack of integration and a poor sense of self.

Personality types and psychiatric disorders have been internationally classified in two main systems—*ICD-10*, by the World Health Organization (2003), and *DSM-IV*, by the American Psychiatric Association (1994). In addition, more recently, classification of personality disorders has been organized into three main clusters. Cluster A personalities are odd or eccentric, referring to paranoid or schizoid individuals; Cluster B personalities are flamboyant or dramatic, and include emotionally unstable, histrionic, antisocial, borderline, and narcissistic personalities; and Cluster C personalities are anxious or fearful, and include those who are anxious, dependent, or obsessive and compulsive. These systems are useful for the child and adult psychiatrist in giving guidance for making diagnoses, although the relevance for the diagnosis of personality disorders is more controversial. Some experts maintain that many of the situations seen in real life are reactions to stressful situations, or problems of "adjustment" to the environment, and as such the medical modeal has only limited relevance to understanding these situations. Indeed, one could add that many of the parents being assessed have had horrific early traumatic experiences, often with a history of being abused, abandoned, or rejected, and as a result their personality development has been interfered with, leaving them having difficulty forming relationships free from violence and abuse. It may be difficult to put a label on their adult personalities; it may be more accurate just to describe the kinds of pattern of relationship personalities that they encounter, which may include problems in keeping their children safe.

Sometimes there is an issue about whether or not a parent has a borderline personality disorder. Borderline conditions constitute a heterogeneous group of diagnostic entities, stretching from conditions where the person may tip into having psychotic experiences when under stress to those where there is more organization of the personality. Psychotic experiences in this context include strong feelings of unreality, delusional or near delusional experiences, and hallucinations. In general, the person with a borderline personality

may display turbulent relationships, moving from partner to partner, with lability of emotion and a poor sense of self. They may shift
between idealization and denigration of people, including professionals, display frequent acting out in self-destructive ways, and
have general difficulty in making emotional contact with others,
including their children. In some women with borderline personalities one can see an intense attachment pattern with primitive idealization, where they cling desperately and unrealistically to men
they idealize, who may well turn out to be potentially dangerous to
them and their children.

Having a diagnosis of personality disorder does not mean being
untreatable, but that some form of specialized psychotherapy is
indicated. There is considerable research evidence, for example in
Chiesa and Fonagy (2000) and Bateman and Fonagy (2001), that
appropriate psychotherapy as an in-patient or day patient is effective for such conditions. Research has also indicated, for example in
Fonagy et al. (1996), that those adults with a borderline personality
who can develop a sense of self reflection during therapy have
more chance of resolving some of their past abuse than those who
do not. Hence the importance of looking for such a capacity in the
initial assessment. Indeed, one could add that one of the most
crucial, yet difficult, tasks for the interviewer is to make some
judgement about the person's capacity to change. It can be impossible to make such a judgement after a one-off interview, and difficult even after a few interviews. It may be necessary to have an
extended period of observation in a day or in-patient setting in
order to clarify how much a parent can use therapeutic resources
and begin to make some fundamental changes. The initial interviewer has to make a judgement about whether or not the parent
shows some encouraging signs of being able to change, such as a
willingness to own up to difficulties, developing insight, and the
cessation of worrying behaviour such as drug or alcohol abuse, as
will be discussed in more detail in the next chapter.

When it comes to interviewing and assessing children and families, a number of different professionals have a role to play, including the child psychiatrist. A child psychotherapist is skilled at
interpreting the child's inner world through the use of play as well
as verbal communications. A clinical psychologist is often trained
in behavioural approaches to working with families, and may, in

addition, have other skills. The child psychiatrist can bring a particular expertise, not only in working with families but also in having an overview of the clinical situation, based on experience in leading multi-disciplinary teams. His or her initial training in medicine and then general psychiatry gives the child psychiatrist a wide knowledge of medical and psychiatric disorders and an ability to assess complex mental states. While skills in assessing children and families overlap with other professionals, the child psychiatrist can have a pivotal role in bringing clarity to complex family problems. While social workers deal with the majority of problem families, the child psychiatrist can deal with the more complex family situations, such as those where a diagnosis of child abuse requires the sifting of considerable clinical evidence, or where the impact on the child of parental difficulties needs careful assessment. The role of the child psychiatrist is particularly relevant when weighing up the advantages and disadvantages of separating children from their parents and placing them with alternative long-term carers. Evaluating the significant harm requiring such a major move can be a difficult exercise. While there is a welfare checklist that the court has to consider in each case, judgements about the capacity of parents to change in their attitudes are far from easy and require full assessments, as the next chapter shows.

The court experience

Preliminary discussion

There is a wide variety of facilities and approaches in the various courts around the country, though with some consistent elements. For example, it is rare to find a court where one can meet and discuss issues in private. Discussion, particularly in the High Court at the Strand, may often have to take place furtively in corridors. Some of the newer courts, such as at Liverpool and Peterborough do have civilized discussion facilities, but many of the older courts do not, or, if they do, there is constant pressure from many other cases for their use. This possibly does reflect, however unconsciously, the essentially adversarial nature of the law. Discussion, if it is to take place—and, indeed, the courts do expect some—has to happen in strained circumstances.

It is often the case that when the expert turns up to give evidence, there is first a discussion with them, wherever that can take place. The purposes of this discussion vary according to the circumstances of the hearing and the nature of the expert's evidence. Although he or she may have been jointly instructed for the purposes of the court, the expert usually appears for one of the parties. In fact, the barrister acting for that party will eventually ask the expert in court relatively friendly questions about their views—this is the examination-in-chief. The other barristers will then cross-examine the expert, and the first barrister can ask the expert further questions. The judge also will usually have some questions of clarification for the expert, in the light of the evidence presented.

Prior to the court appearance itself, it is common to have a preliminary discussion with a barrister and their solicitor, if present, and subsequently any other professionals such as social workers or another expert. Usually this discussion is helpful, not only to bring the expert up-to-date with developments at court, but also to begin a process of negotiation and resolution of conflict between the parties. The expert can often be used as a go-between in order to come up with an acceptable plan of action, a basis for rehabilitation, or a care plan, which is then presented to the judge, with or without the expert having to appear in the witness box. If all parties are in agreement with what is drawn up, then the expert may not have to appear. Sometimes a judge likes to see the expert in court in order to acknowledge the work they have done; others may even have a brief chat from the bench about the agreement, just to make sure the expert does not have to be examined. Others are happy for the expert to go back to their clinic work without being seen in court.

In some courts the expert may occupy a room where individual barristers can come to them for their views, and then go back to their clients, and then everyone may finally agree to meet in order to pull the plan together before going into court to tell the judge what has been happening. In the High Court this usually happens in the corridor. Sometimes only the lawyers meet to thrash out some compromise, and then they come to the expert for a clinical view. At other times matters can only be settled by the expert going on the witness stand. Even if there is a general agreement on most points, there may be some points that can only be resolved after cross-examination, such as the extent and intensity of contact between parents and children.

Where there are other experts, it is to be hoped that there has already been a meeting, either in person or on the phone, in order to clarify areas of agreement and disagreement. However, with particularly tricky cases the experts may have to meet at court for further discussion, and their views may be continually sought as the situation develops; for example, if a parent no longer wishes to contest expert views or if new evidence comes to light.

Occasionally, several experts may have to be present in order to clarify their different positions, particularly where one expert disagrees with all the others. This happened in one case where a father had a previous history of sexual molestation of young children. Most of the expert opinion was that he should not remain in the home with his new baby, particularly as the mother denied that there was any risk to the child. Two experts on paedophilia agreed that the father still had active paedophilic fantasies that had not responded to treatment interventions. However, one psychologist who had been seeing him disagreed with this view and thought that he was now safe around children. Because of the understandably worrying nature of his problems, all the experts, including myself and another child psychiatrist, had to spend the day in court trying to see if there were any possibility of a unanimous agreement. Because this was not possible, all parties had to be cross-examined. In fact, the father was not allowed to remain in the marital home.

Sometimes the expert turns up in court to find a complete change of situation. If there is going to be a long hearing lasting three or more days, expert witnesses usually do not appear on the first day, which is often taken up with an introduction to the issues. By the time the expert arrives, there may have been new developments as a result of what has gone on in court. For example, in the following case, I appeared to support the rehabilitation of a mother and her young child. The mother had long-standing emotional and personality problems, with alcoholism being a major factor in the past. She seemed to have been off the alcohol for at least a year, and there was no evidence of drinking while she was being assessed over some weeks. There was also a history of violent relationships with men, but she seemed reasonably in touch with her child and it was felt that rehabilitation was worth trying, though she was not very keen on having therapy as she felt, wrongly in the professionals' view, that her problems were not as great as the other parents at the Cassel.

When I arrived for a one-day hearing to discuss my recommendations, to my surprise there was no one available to discuss the situation. I asked to see the mother's barrister but was told he was unavailable. I was told that the other workers were around somewhere, but I could not find where. The whole situation seemed bizarre and I was wondering if I had the wrong day in my diary when, by chance, I saw the mother's barrister. The latter explained rather perfunctorily, that the mother no longer wished to take up the recommended treatment. The mother was also not available for any discussion about this.

I was finally able to meet the Social Services, the Guardian, and the independent expert in a room, where I discussed the situation with them. They had all been sceptical about the mother's capacity to change. I eventually came to the view that they were right and I was wrong, and that clearly there was nothing I could do to help the situation. It did seem that the mother's barrister was unhelpful; it was difficult to understand what had happened between him and his client but there was nothing more to be done. I was not even asked to give any evidence, which again was rather strange.

When, a few months later, I turned up for the final hearing, the mother had been drinking heavily again, had not turned up for contact visits, and was also involved in domestic violence once more. She soon agreed for the child to go for adoption as she was clearly in no position to take on his care. The last I heard about this sad situation was that a year or so later, the mother was in prison for murdering her boyfriend. Of course, it was in retrospect rather a relief that she had not been taken on for treatment, although it was also difficult not to have the thought that if she had been willing to accept help, she and her victim might have been saved their terrible fate.

Dealing with courts

The overall approach to be recommended in dealing with meetings at court and with the various workers is to listen calmly and attentively to all the views. This is the best way of dealing with the often conflicting views of the various parties. It is also best not to get angry, unless you are kept waiting unnecessarily, which still happens from time to time. Coming to court means that the expert has to cancel or, if given enough notice, rearrange appointments with other patients. However, the expert sometimes does not know until the day before whether or not they are needed in court, a most unsatisfactory situation. The High Court and the Principal Registry are usually good about accommodating the expert and making sure they are not kept waiting. This is not so often the case with courts outside London, perhaps because they have so much other business to conduct in the day.

In general, lawyers and the courts seem to have a completely different attitude to time from that of the clinician. While a clinician has to book appointments well in advance and generally thinks weeks and even months ahead, and although a court has to be booked many months in advance, some lawyers seem to think the expert can be immediately available, or that a family can be seen and dealt with at once. For example, there are a number of occasions when my secretary is telephoned directly from court by a lawyer wanting my views about whether or not I can see a family. While there is no objection to such a request, my secretary often finds that the lawyer wants instant replies, and can become annoyed when she explains that some notice may be needed and that I may have to read through some of the documents first before committing myself. The strange thing is that once there is an agreement to oblige, it can then be very difficult to get hold of these same lawyers; for example, to discuss the case or, much later, to retrieve a bill for services rendered.

Sometimes the dynamics between the lawyers reflects the family's pathology—which some very "logical" lawyers find difficult to understand. For example, an expert was giving evidence in a difficult case with an aggressive mother who was unable to provide a safe environment for her young child, despite a considerable amount of input, probably because her terrible childhood experiences of abuse and neglect were just too great to be resolved in some way quickly enough to enable her to take on the full time care of her child. However, she also had some good points and a desperate, if unrealistic, wish to keep her child, the expert noted the almost exact correspondence between his own experience of how he had to make a final and very difficult clinical decision with all the various workers present and how the lawyers were lining themselves up in similar ways in court, with an attempt to delay any decision making. One barrister was particularly outraged that the expert was not sticking to the facts in the case, accusing him of being merely speculative. While granting that it was important to curb a tendency to make speculative comments on the witness stand, the expert did point out to him that it was rare to find a fact without some kind of feeling attached to it, but the barrister remained unconvinced.

One could say that at these times the expert may find themselves representing the presence of *feelings*, while the court process tends, on the surface at least, to be focusing on *facts*. The point to make here is that feelings, and often very disturbing ones, are flying around the court, and that lawyers, as much as mental health professionals, need to take notice of them.

Giving expert evidence

Being in the witness box and giving evidence about difficult family situations requires a technique. Mr Justice Wall (2000) has given some very useful guidelines to follow. For example, he recommends that you should answer the questions put to you, take your time, try to keep to the point, and never try to get into an argument with the questioner.

Thus, if the expert does not understand a question, or has forgotten it, they should say so. If necessary, they should ask the judge for help. In fact, it is absolutely vital to make sure that there is good communication with the judge. Sometimes flattery may be needed to ensure this happens. Judges and barristers in family cases do not wear wigs and gowns, but the court process is still formal and there is a need to show respect to the court and to the judge if one's evidence is going to be taken seriously. A reasonably decent, though not too flashy, suit is appropriate to maintain gravitas.

When arriving at the witness box, try to make yourself as comfortable as possible. After taking the oath, ask for some water if there is none. If there is no chair, ask for it to be found. Often the judge invites you to sit or stand, depending on what you wish.

Sitting is more comfortable and can appear to be more modest. Standing gives the impression that you want to be at the same level as the barristers, who do stand when speaking. However, there are a few occasions where it can be useful to stand; for example, if you wish to peer down from an appropriate height at a barrister asking difficult questions, but this is a risky tactic only to be tried by the very experienced witness, for barristers are expert at dealing with intimidating witnesses. Overall, try to create a setting for yourself where you can think. Try to appear to be comfortable and at ease, even if you are not; be confident, but not cocky.

Try to speak as genuinely as you can about what you think and feel about a family you have seen. Do not try to be too clever—barristers are much better than you at being clever in court. If the clinician sticks to his own field then he or she is on safer ground. Stick to the clinical issues, leaving the lawyers to argue about the law, except on the rare occasions when you are more up-to-date with a recent judgement. It is important to agree with a point made when you do agree, and to disagree when necessary, giving justifications for the disagreement.

For much of the time the parents are present in court while you are giving evidence, and this means that you must take account of their hearing what may be very critical remarks. An appropriate restraint is vital, but there may be times when the cross-examination entails having to spell out a parent's failings, which can be very upsetting to them, even though they have had sight of all the reports before the case begins and may know, intellectually at least, what is going to come up.

A particularly tricky situation may arise if the parent undertakes their own cross-examination, which has happened to me on only one occasion. This was with a very difficult mother who had dismissed several teams of lawyers, as they would not do what she wished. One of the main points about my own evidence was that the mother would not listen and would bombard others with her own fixed views. I was very careful to be polite, and to make allowances for the mother conducting her own case. When one of her questions continued for nearly ten minutes I decided not to interrupt her, which I would have done had she been a barrister, but to let her have her say. My only comment then was that she had just displayed very clearly in her bombardment what I had described in my report.

Occasionally the expert has to address in court the views of another expert opinion that he or she may have considered either incompetent or irrelevant, and this can be very tricky. There are a number of retired professionals who, no longer working in the NHS, have the time to spend in court and who are thus often used as experts. Some of them are excellent, while others have dubious and eccentric views. Sometimes one meets an expert who has a pet theory, or only one approach to everything, or has found the answer to every child's problem. The best way to deal with views one finds incompetent is to quietly and systematically argue why and how the views are untenable in that particular case, hopefully with some research evidence to back up one's own opinion. Having to meet such experts at court and talk to them can certainly test out one's own diplomatic skills to the limit at times.

Having tried to be as cooperative and respectful as possible, and having followed the guidelines for giving evidence, the expert may still find themselves at the receiving end of aggression, both from the barristers, which one expects, but also occasionally from the judge, who may dislike any expert, or that particular expert if their beliefs and views conflict. For example, one judge clearly believed that all teenage mothers appearing before him should have their babies removed at birth and put up for adoption and he gave an expert a very difficult time when he argued, successfully in the end, that a particular teenager should have the chance of an assessment of her mothering capacities. In fact, the expert was so enraged by his views that he suggested that this was the argument for eugenics promoted by the Nazis. Thus, there are times when the expert just cannot keep a lid on their feelings, but this is not to be recommended for those beginning their court experience. Instead, the better technique is to keep cool and stick to the clinical facts.

If bombarded by questions, it is best to try to slow down the answers, to take even more time than usual and to allow longish silences in order both to think and to disrupt the barrister's style. The point being made is that it is not always the case that the expert is treated fairly and courteously by the barristers or the judge. It is certainly not always the case when the judge intervenes to prevent cross-examination being personal or offensive, as they should and as Wall (2000, p. 66) urges. The fact is the expert occasionally needs to marshal all their wiles and all their defensive techniques to deal with the ensuing battle and they need to find their own way of surviving this experience. If you are asked the same question over and over, but in slightly different ways, you can say you have already answered that question several times. You may decline to look much at the barrister and address your answers to the judge. You can certainly ask the judge for help, if they have not given it to you already. Being firm, clear, unbullied, and calm is the best way of convincing a sceptical court of one's credibility. Assessing the credibility of the expert witness comes into the realm of informal personality assessment, though from the judge's position. Obviously, what the expert witness says and how they express themselves will determine how the judge weighs up their credibility. Clear answers backed up by the clinical evidence will be more convincing than mere assertion. Knowledge of relevant research evidence can be helpful, though it does not make up for poor interviewing technique. The way that the witness comes across as a person and how they deal with cross-examination will be crucial to what opinion the Judge forms of the reliability of their views. Indeed, the whole set-up is a form of appraisal. If a witness refuses to concede points that are made, if they stick to their views regardless, then they will come across as rigid and opinionated rather than having a valid opinion. Being authoritative is different from being omnipotent, and thus it is important for the credible expert witness to make it clear when a particular issue falls outside their own level of expertise or knowledge.

What is evidence?

Evidence in law appears to be straightforward, in that it refers to what proves or disproves any matter of fact, the truth of which is subjected to judicial investigation. Facts can be proved by direct evidence such as that of witnesses, or by indirect evidence as to other facts from which the facts at issue are inferred. The evidence in family law may come from oral statements in court or from written statements. One of the primary tasks of the judge is to decide the facts upon which he must ultimately base his decision; that is, the judge first of all makes "findings of fact" on the balance of probabilities. Facts may well be contested, and it is then up to the judge, with the help of his or her own experience, sometimes aided by expert opinion, to decide what facts are most plausible. The judge then applies the facts to the statutory tests; for example, to determine whether or not a child has suffered significant harm, or is out of parental control.

An order of various kinds is made when not to do so would lead to the child suffering "significant harm". This refers to emotional, physical, or sexual abuse and maltreatment, or impairment of physical or mental health, or developmental problems attributable to parental failure. The judge applies the "threshold test", making a decision as to whether or not the facts establish that the threshold criteria of significant harm have been met. Expert opinion can be crucial at this point to establish whether or not the children have suffered harm over an extended period.

Predicting risk of future harm can be very difficult, particularly when it is a question of emotional harm. While a finding of physical or sexual abuse is straightforward, in the sense that there is clearly a risk of recurrence, without some kind of intervention, that of emotional harm is more complex, and usually requires evidence of ongoing emotional disturbance in the children, including severe emotional and behavioural problems, failure to thrive in babies, or clear evidence of severe and ongoing neglect.

The judge will then decide on the outcome; for example, whether or not a Care Plan is appropriate for a child, whether or not rehabilitation with their parent should be attempted, whether or not contact with one parent should be maintained. Expert opinion will aid the judge in coming to a decision, but it is up to the judge to decide whether or not the expert views are consistent with his or her own view of matters, which will include a judgement of the plausibility of the expert's evidence, as well as some informal weighing up of the parent's personality, their genuineness, their willingness to concede facts that are found, and how they come across in the witness box, if they appear.

While legal evidence appears to be straightforward, in that there are procedures for presenting and examining it, the finding and presenting of clinical evidence is far from straightforward. What kind of clinical picture emerges from the expert's interviews reflects their own approach, and in this sense is a subjective process, however much the expert sticks to accepted guidelines, along the lines presented in the next chapter.

So-called "evidence-based medicine" has become a standard for justifying clinical views. This refers to external clinical evidence from systematic research. The so-called "gold standard" for evidence is the randomized, controlled trial (RCT), or the meta-analysis of several randomized trials. However, as Philip Graham, a former Professor of Child Psychiatry at Great Ormond Street Hospital, has persuasively argued, a reliance on evidence of this kind inapplicable to the field of child psychiatry (Graham, 2000). RCT studies have only limited application where children are concerned, because they focus on symptoms rather than human predicaments, which are the main concern of clinicians.

Also, diagnoses in the child field are complex, and often do not fit into clear research diagnosis criteria. Graham adds that where it is possible to validate findings by an evidence-based approach, this can be valuable, but it is not the only way to look at evidence. Qualitative studies as well as clinical audit can often be more relevant. One could add that a major problem with the RCT approach is that it is designed to eliminate observer involvement, but that in this field such involvement is fundamental, as one is dealing with the complexities of human relationships. As Williams and Garner (2002) argue in another paper on the limitations of evidence-based medicine, sophisticated clinical expertise with regard to an individual patient should be balanced with an evidence base derived from a group. Too much emphasis on a narrow range of acceptable evidence oversimplifies the complex range of clinical care. While medicine has to be rooted in science, doctors are also healers. Evidence from human relationships requires some form of narrative account of what took place in the various interactions between the people involved. Narrative evidence would then seem to be more relevant to this field than the evidence from detached positive science, though the latter can be useful when looking at the overall outcome of interventions among groups of patients. Indeed, it could be argued that one needs to tackle the nature of clinical evidence from a variety of standpoints, varying from a positivist position requiring empirical verification of facts, as takes place in the first stage of the judicial decision-making process, to the more interpretive position, where the clinician and family interact. In the latter approach there is still the need to examine the details of a clinical presentation, in order to judge their relevance and capacity to convince, their plausibility in the context of the issues under consideration.

CHAPTER TWO

Assessing families

Assessment as process

Making clinical assessments of families is a complex task, requiring attention to details of the family's history, observing present relationships, looking at the developmental needs of the child, making a judgement about parenting capacity as well as the parents' personality, while all the time trying to see, often through a mass of paperwork and information of varying reliability, what is in the child's best interests. Maintaining a capacity to think and reflect is essential to the assessor, and finding such a capacity, however limited, in the family being assessed is a hopeful sign of the possibility of change. After all, a fundamental aim of assessment is to see how much a family is capable of change. But assessing change can be difficult, provoke very different views in professionals, and may need a certain amount of time and an open attitude of mind, the latter being particularly difficult when both the family and the professional network have already made up theirs.

Allowing a picture of what is right for the child to emerge from the assessment process is not an easy matter. Sometimes the right clinical picture emerges only during the writing of the report, when all the threads begin to come together. And, of course, the clinical assessment, however important, is only advisory to the court; which will use it as such in formulating its own assessment.

Assessment is not an end in itself, but, as the Department of Health states in its guide to the assessment of children in need, consists of a process:

> which will lead to the improvement in the well-being or outcomes for a child or young person. The conclusion of an assessment should result in:
>
> ● an analysis of the needs of the child and the parenting capacity to respond appropriately to those needs within their family context;
> ● identification of whether and; if so, where intervention will be required to secure the well-being of the child or young person;
> ● a realistic plan of action including services to be provided detailing who has responsibility for action, a timetable and a process of review. [DoH, 2000, p. 53]

Thus, assessment should be the first stage in a process leading to some kind of helpful intervention. The Department of Health's guide provides a useful model, which will be the basis of points subsequently made in this chapter, of how to keep children safe and promote their welfare by looking at three elements:

● the child's developmental needs
● the capacities of parents or caregivers to respond appropriately to those needs
● the impact of wider family and environmental factors on parenting capacity and the children.

Unfortunately, it is often the case, particularly outside London, that services are geared up to short-term assessments but can offer little in the way of treatment interventions. Making a "realistic" plan of action often means taking account of this massive gap in current resources. It is not simply a question of lack of money being available for such work, but also a great absence of expertise and training.

In addition, it can be very difficult trying to treat the more seriously disturbed families; it takes time, requires skill in managing the risks, and is emotionally disturbing to the professionals involved, who thus need considerable support and skilled supervision to be able to cope with the demands of the work. Sometimes a family can cause such immense strain in the professional network that one may encounter a series of workers who have only been able to tolerate working with them for short periods. Occasionally one may even encounter situations where one or more social worker has been made ill by having to work with a particular family. Thus, one can not overemphasize the enormous strain that this kind of work produces in professionals, and hence the need for support. The strain can come not only from having to be at the receiving end of verbal and occasionally physical abuse from difficult parents, but also from being a witness to the suffering of the children.

While most family assessments in the field of child mental health do not involve the courts, two kinds of assessment that do will be covered:

1. Specialist assessment of multi problem families, which usually require a multidisciplinary approach, and which frequently address the issue of whether or not a child should be with their parents, and, if so, what needs to be done to allow this to happen.
2. Assessment of limited issues, such as advice about residence and contact arrangements, where the expert may act mainly alone, with the occasional participation of another expert. While there is much overlap between these kinds of assessment, there are also specific issues relevant to each.

Assessment as therapy

It is good practice in both kinds of assessment described above to aim to make them as therapeutic as possible. Rather than merely eliciting clinical facts in some dry way, it is advisable for the expert to try to look anew at the family's situation, and to convey the impression that, however many people the family have seen before, he or she wishes to hear from them what they have to say in their own words, even though confidentiality is inevitably compromised by the expert having to report what they say. That is, while the expert has a certain technical knowledge of the field of child and family problems, as well as adult personality issues, and will use that during the assessment, he or she should start from a position that the meeting with the family concerns basic human issues about the quality of their lives. While what has happened before they come to see the expert is part of the clinical picture, and though the often extensive documentation preceding the assessment provides the context for any clinical opinion, what happens when the family is in the room will be crucial in making a judgement about what should happen. That is, the clinical judgement will concern the quality and pattern of the family's ways of relating between themselves and with others.

Some families have been seen many times by different professionals, and the best approach may be to convey that the meeting is a chance to see things anew. For other families the meeting, or meetings, may be the first opportunity, especially for the children, to tell their story in a sympathetic environment. Many of the families, particularly those being considered for a day or residential assessment, are highly disadvantaged socially, often with housing and financial problems, and with a long history of emotional as well as social deprivation. They may be deeply suspicious of the authorities, whom they see as threatening and uncaring. While a good lawyer can help to prepare them for the interview, it is inevitable that the expert is seen as coming from another world far from theirs. The expert being a doctor does help to overcome some of their fears, as, despite recent scandals, most doctors are seen as trustworthy, a figure to whom one can tell problems.

The approach being described is essentially about working within a special kind of relationship, one that is based upon a psychoanalytical understanding of relationships. It is about making contact with people in difficult circumstances. It requires patient and highly skilled listening; attention to anxieties, defences, and the subtleties of personality, as well as an openness to the unknown. Quite often the expert has to face calmly and thoughtfully very disturbing feelings coming at them from the family members, a skill that is indispensable when undertaking an assessment of a disturbed family. The ability to withstand the impact of powerful and conflicting emotions is also very helpful when dealing with disturbed families over several years. This is a field, as already mentioned in the opening chapter, where professionals easily "burn out", because they cannot deal with the emotional impact of the work. For this reason, it is essential for the expert to have somewhere, such as a small continuous professional development (CPD) group, where they can talk about clinical work in confidence and with respected colleagues.

However, despite any amount of experience and support, it can still be very difficult to make good contact with families who have been through the child care network, as they often feel persecuted by those they have seen, particularly if they have had a child removed. Professionals can become inured from feeling much sympathy for the parents, after seeing family after family with a long and repeated history of parental neglect, abuse, and deprivation. It is tempting to write the parents off as hopeless, particularly if they are resentful about being helped. It certainly saves the considerable time and effort that would be required to make a full assessment of the family's capacities, including whether not there is any hope of change.

The sense of persecution persists throughout this kind of work and at various sites in the assessment process, within the family and among the professionals working with them. It is commonly a reflection of the parents' persecuting inner world, which is projected to a greater or lesser extent on to the professional network. A fear of dependency is also a frequent theme in such families, which can manifest itself in pushing away professional help, as well as in difficulties responding to their children's emotional pain.

One should not, however, minimize the real persecution that deprived families experience as a result of feeling powerless in the hands of a complex and frightening care system. Social services will at times have to act as parents to the children when their own parents have failed to look after them safely and effectively. It is obvious that this will cause resentment in the parents. But at the same time, once the authorities act as parents in this way, they will arouse, usually unconsciously, yearnings in the actual parents to be looked after as well, in a way that they probably did not experience earlier in their life. Yet the parents fight such yearnings and deny any sense of dependency on the authorities, complaining instead of feeling persecuted. It is even more persecuting for them to acknowledge their dependency needs, which is ultimately essential if future rehabilitation is to succeed. Both the parents and their workers can become locked into a battle, rather than each side facing the difficult feelings stirred up by the necessity of intervening.

Getting to first base: acknowledging responsibility

When assessing a family, the expert should convey that their views are their own and that they are not, as it were, "in the pay" of social services, a common fear. That is, the expert should convey their *independence*. However, they should also be clear, where appropriate, that they take seriously what other professionals have found. This may be most obvious where the parents refuse to acknowledge any responsibility for what they have done to their children, despite extensive evidence of their actions. At this point it may be necessary to turn to any clear forensic evidence of past non-accidental injury and confront the parents with what has been found. Such confrontations are necessary, in the adversarial system of child protection in which we work in this country. However, as the final chapter describes in more detail, one could argue that if there were more emphasis on conciliation, then it might well be the case that more families would own up to risky behaviour without coercion, particularly if they felt that it was in their interests to do so, and if they felt that they might get help as a result rather than lose their children. So long as treatment resources are few and far between, the families may well feel that there is no point in cooperating with the authorities, because the latter cannot offer any appropriate therapeutic interventions.

Challenging the family at this point about their lack of acknowledgement may have different outcomes, such as initial denial, or owning up at the last minute, as shown in the following example.

Some years ago an expert saw a couple with a baby who maintained that the severe physical injuries their first child had sustained were not caused by them, even though there was clear forensic evidence that the child, who had gone for adoption, had suffered non-accidental injuries. The referral had indicated that there was something hopeful about the couple, despite the history. Mother came across as more in touch with her emotions, despite her difficult history—she had been abandoned by her own unstable mother, and had been brought up in a series of foster homes, in two of which she had been sexually abused. She had had a very troubled adolescence, and had soon become pregnant. There was, in fact, something likeable about her in the way that she conveyed that she had tried to keep hope alive during her difficult life, and she was also good with her baby, who was in a foster home. The couple had regular contact with the baby, and there were no reported difficulties during contact visits.

Her partner came across as a lonely, isolated man, prone to sudden outbursts of rage; he had been brought up in his own family, but with a violent and alcoholic father who had beaten up his wife and children. He minimized the unhappiness he had suffered as a child, and they both continued to maintain that their previous child could not have been injured by either of them, despite it having sustained serious fractures, including a twisting injury to one leg, which could only have been done by someone intent on injury.

While there were some positive aspects, particularly in the way that the couple related to their baby, what was deeply worrying was the obvious potential risk to their child of suffering a non-accidental injury, given the fact that there was no acknowledgement of the past abuse. Professional experience and clinical evidence points to the high risk of repeated abuse in families who do not acknowledge responsibility for their actions (see, for example, Bentovim, 1992). Hence it would be a very risky undertaking to attempt further assessment or treatment of such a family without some shift in their attitude. One could not guarantee that the child would be reasonably safe from harm.

Thus, the expert put to the couple that there was nothing he could do to help them, given their attitude of denial of their obvious difficulties. They persisted in maintaining their position, and, with some resentment, left the meeting, with the baby returning to its foster home. However, an hour or so later, they returned, wanting to see the interviewer again. By chance he was available, and in the second interview the father owned up to injuring the child and the mother owned up to knowing about it.

Being faced with a stark choice of owning up to the truth or losing their second child, they finally opened up, and, as a result, were eventually successfully treated.

Not all assessments of this kind end happily; a number of families who continue to deny past and present difficulties feel bitter and resentful about being turned down for help. The assessor is then seen as just one in a long line of unhelpful and prejudiced professionals.

Other parents may come to the assessment meeting after having owned up to injuring a child, but only after some time, and that can create difficulties for the assessor. If the parent has, for example, only owned up their actions during the court case, then one is naturally suspicious that this is not a genuine acknowledgement of responsibility, and that it was made out of fear or as part of some legal ploy. At the same time, some parents can only really see the consequences of their actions once the court process has got under way.

It can also be difficult to assign responsibility for injuries where there is a couple where one parent owns up to the abuse and the other does not and claims to be innocent.

While this may well be the case, the assessor has to try to establish the quality of the couple's relationship, how much communication takes place between them, and how it was possible for one parent to abuse their child without the apparent knowledge of the other parent.

An example of owning up at the last minute is shown in the following case history.

An expert saw a couple with their young child after the mother had finally owned up to fracturing the child's arm on two occasions. The context for the assessment was that forensic evidence for the first injury was equivocal; it took place in the context of a young and anxious mother having difficulty coping with her first child, and an attempt was made to work with the couple in the community. It was only after the second and more serious injury that measures were taken to remove the child into foster care and the court process begun. Only after some months, as the final hearing to decide the child's future approached, was there any shift in the owning of responsibility for the injuries. All along, the father had denied involvement in the injuries, though clearly he had not picked up what was happening at home. But the mother agreed that she had hurt the child in a fit of frustration, when the child kept crying without a break. There were also deep family divisions on both the father and mother's side, with the couple in the middle, rather like Romeo and Juliet with their feuding families on their backs.

Several experts were involved in the case, and there was concern about the safety of the child, but uncertainty about whether or not the couple were treatable. It was only when the family were admitted to a residential unit that the picture became clearer, as then the marital violence came into the open. The father, who had come across as quiet and reasonable, turned out to be deeply denigrating of his wife, and had hit her on a few occasions. He also maintained that the injuries were solely his wife's fault, and that he could not be blamed for them, even though he had clearly ignored the fact that his child must have been in excessive pain for at least several days before the first injury was discovered. The mother clearly had great problems in containing her frustration with her child, but the marital relationship was not safe for children, and hence the father had his own responsibility for the injuries. In the end, the couple separated as a result of being at the unit, and their child was adopted by one set of grandparents, so that there was limited contact with the parents.

Responsibility for injuries to a child may never be clarified, or may continue to remain a grey area, which is particularly worrying.

Sometimes a case may demonstrate confused responsibility, such as the one detailed below. This concerned an articulate, middle-class couple whose youngest child had been badly injured. Neither parent would admit to causing the injury, though a judge had decided that it was more likely than not that the mother had done so. There was never any admission from her of any guilt, and partly because the judge's finding of fact was not absolutely clear, the parents continued to maintain their innocence.

The mother conceded that she might have winded the child rather too vigorously, but that would never have accounted for the injuries. The father did think he might have hurt the child by mistake when he was changing its nappy and fell, but that was as far any admission of guilt went. Because of the level of uncertainty for the local authority, they asked for an expert assessment.

The couple's relationships, both with each other and with the staff, became a main focus of the assessment. They revealed considerable hostility to any case workers, and resisted any serious attempt to understand what was happening in the family. The expert could see that there was also great hostility between the couple, but they denied it. It seemed pretty clear to the expert that the injury to the child took place in the context of that unacknowledged mutual hostility, but the couple were unwilling to concede any difficulties. Nothing changed at the final hearing, but their child remained within the extended family, with the parents sharing the care.

It was only some years later that the local authority asked the expert to see the father, in order to assess whether or not he could take on the full-time care of the girl who had been injured in the past. He and his wife had separated soon after the court case, and he admitted that the workers had been right about the mutual hostility. He was now certain that his wife had injured the child, and was very guilty about his part in covering up what had happened. The mother, meanwhile, had withdrawn from the care of her daughter, and the father had been effectively looking after her full-time. The expert did agree that this should continue and that the father had moved on greatly since he was first seen several years previously.

Step by step assessment

The papers

GENERAL POINTS

Not surprisingly, the amount and complexity of the papers usually reflects the nature of the issues surrounding a family assessment. Thus, when the expert is asked for a view about whether or not a child should have contact with an absent parent, or should change contact arrangements, the papers are usually fairly brief and straightforward. The vital letter of instruction is usually to the point, even if both sets of lawyers cannot always agree on joint instructions, reflecting in this case their clients' own rigid positions. However, with the more complex cases, with extensive involvement of several agencies, one may be faced with several boxes of documents, much of which it is not necessary to read. For example, there is little point in being given page after page of judicial orders when one page with a summary will do. Given the daunting mass of documentation—usually the more there is, the more the anxiety and confusion exists about what should be done—what can the poor clinician do to make sense of the referral?

A really good *letter of instruction* is an absolute requirement. Without a clear summary of the history and the issues, there is no point in trying to wade through the papers. The absence of such a summary already indicates that there is either an extreme amount of ambivalence about asking for an assessment, or else an inability in the professional network to think clearly about the family, or both. While Wall (2000, p. 24) recommends the expert to tell the parties where a letter of instruction is inadequate or where more documentation is required, asking for better instructions may be necessary but may also unduly delay matters, especially as most assessments have to stick to a strict timetable, and such an inquiry will not necessarily lead to any further action. The expert could justifiably refuse to see a family if there were no instructions, just a bundle of documents—which happens from time to time. In that case, the expert should send back a clear letter to the instructing lawyers and the social services, giving the reasons for the refusal to see the family, and requesting them to send back a good letter of instruction as soon as possible.

Experts should also decline to take instructions if they feel that the issues under consideration are beyond their own area of expertise; for example, if they were in child psychiatry but were being asked to comment on pathological reports, or if they were asked to give a paediatric opinion. In that case, the expert needs to send back a letter explaining the importance of looking for the right expert and indicating who that should be.

Sometimes the family mental health expert may indicate that they have little experience in a particular field, such as the assessment of the state of mind of a suspected murderer, but the parties have still wanted their views as someone with a knowledge of personality disorder.

The issue of the timetable for the assessment usually arises from the beginning. The expert should only agree to see the family if he or she can comply with the timetable for when the court has to receive the report. If this is not possible, it must be made plain from the start, so that either another expert can be found or the lawyers can return to court in order to ask for a revised timetable.

Sometimes the time factor can be persecuting for the expert and his or her secretary. For example, there are occasions when an extreme impatience to receive an answer from the expert about their willingness to, say, look at some papers, is conveyed to the expert's secretary, with badgering and even occasionally downright rudeness—an answer has to be given then and there, with the lawyer probably in court at the time. They want to know if the expert can see a family, when they can do so and when they will be available for court, all at the drop of a hat, as if the expert had nothing else to do.

Sending one's secretary on an assertiveness course can be helpful in dealing with such bullying tactics. Sometimes a letter to the lawyer pointing out how unreasonable they were may be in order, including asking for an apology. However, the basic problem is probably one of different time scales and institutional worlds in which lawyers and clinicians generally work. The clinician has to set up appointments weeks and even months in advance; they do not work to a "last minute" timetable, except in the rare cases of an emergency, such as when dealing with a suicidal patient. Barristers are used to receiving their briefs just before they have to appear in court, while clinicians are used to having their evenings free to be with their family.

KINDS OF INSTRUCTION

The expert may be instructed by only one party, or may be a single joint expert (SJE), or may be a joint expert along with one or more other experts.

An expert may be instructed by one party separately, such as a parent, because the other parties consider that an expert is unnecessary; for example, if the Guardian and the social services are clearly of the view that a child should be removed from their parents.

The parents' lawyer may then be the only one to hold out any hope for the parents. While this is acceptable for the expert themselves, the problem with being instructed by one party is that it is then difficult, though not impossible, for that expert to be jointly instructed at a later date. What the expert recommends and whether or not the other parties agree with their views will, of course, influence how the case progresses.

The advantage of being jointly instructed is that this usually implies that the expert's view is respected by the various parties, and that there is some agreement about what issues need to be addressed and by whom. When the expert's view is sufficiently authoritative, and is accepted by all parties, a considerable amount of court time and legal costs can be saved.

The disadvantage of being a single joint expert is that a difficult case may impose a considerable burden on the expert, who in fact may welcome another view or discussion with another expert about what to recommend. Joint instruction can also cause delay if the opinion of one expert clashes with that of another, or if the opinion of the single joint expert is challenged by one party who then insists on a second opinion. As will be described later, meetings before the court hears all the evidence in a case are essential when there are joint experts, but this can cause considerable delay. While it is good practice to have these meetings face to face and as soon as possible after reports have been written, in reality setting up these meetings can be a nightmare, because of the difficulty of finding mutually acceptable times to meet, as well as the fact that communication between different offices with different secretarial resources can make matters even more difficult to resolve. It might be better to timetable a meeting of experts when the original instructions go out, rather than wait until later.

There are now clear guidelines, produced in 2002 by the President of the Family Division's Ancillary Relief Advisory Group, for instructing a single joint expert. According to the President of the Family Division's practice direction of 25 May 2000 [2000] 1 FLR 997), where expert evidence is sought, parties should, if possible, agree upon a single joint expert whom they can jointly instruct, in order to save time and money. Before instructions are given, the parties should obtain confirmation from the proposed expert:

(a)   that there is no conflict of interest;
(b)   that the matter is within the range of expertise of the expert;
(c)   that the expert is available to provide the report within a specified time scale;
(d)   of the expert's availability for attendance at any dates that are known to be relevant;

(e)   of any periods when the expert will not be available;
(f)   as to the expert's fee rate, basis of charging, other terms of business, and best estimate of likely fee;
(g)   if applicable, that the expert will accept instructions on a publicly funded basis.

The parties will also need to agree about the sharing out of the fee. In fact, this causes the most headaches for the expert, as it is often difficult to obtain payment for services when the fee is shared by more than one party. I have certainly experienced more than one occasion of having to pursue one or more sets of solicitors for up to a year before they release the fee, while another set involved in the same case pays within a reasonable time frame. Thus, it is important for the expert to have good secretarial back-up, and to pay the secretary extra money for this frustrating and time consuming "debt collecting" activity. Local authorities usually pay quite quickly and without any fuss, probably because they do not put payments through legal aid.

Where the court then directs a report by the SJE, the order should, according to the practice guide:

(a)   if the SJE has already been instructed, adopt the instructions already given or make such amendments to the instructions as the court thinks fit;
(b)   identify the SJE;
(c)   specify the task that the SJE has to perform;
(d)   provide that the instructions are to be contained in a jointly agreed letter;
(e)   specify the time within which the letter of instruction is to be sent;
(f)   specify the date by which the report must be produced;
(g)   provide for the date by which written questions may be put to the SJE and the date by which they must be answered;
(h)   make any such provision as to the SJE's fees which the court thinks appropriate.

The joint instructions should include any basic relevant information, any assumptions to be made, the principally known issues, and the specific questions to be answered, as well as copies of court orders and any documents, appropriately and legibly ordered and indexed.

Once the SJE has received the letter of instruction, or at any later date, they should raise any issues they think relevant, such as lack of clarity or completeness, and any modifications to their fee that may ensue. Sometimes the letter of instruction makes clear that more work than originally anticipated by the expert may be necessary, and hence that an increased fee will be charged. Before proceeding with the work, the expert needs to check that this is acceptable. For example, if the instructions state that the expert needs to see several hours of videotaped interviews of a family, rather than just read some transcripts, this will entail several hours of extra activity that need to be priced.

All communications by the SJE should be addressed to the various parties, and the SJE should keep all parties informed of what they intend doing, e.g., by copying all correspondence to each party.

Unless with specific agreement, the SJE should not attend any meeting or conference that is not a joint one, in order that their neutrality is maintained.

The report of the SJE should be served simultaneously on all parties.

If there are major problems with the SJE being able to maintain their neutrality or able to do the job because of, for example, obstruction or any other reason, the SJE may have to resign the joint appointment. If so, they need to give a concise statement of their reasons for so doing.

WHAT THE LETTER OF INSTRUCTION SHOULD INCLUDE

As Wall (2000, p. 24) states, it is of the utmost importance that the expert is properly and fully instructed, and that they have access to all the material that is necessary for the proper preparation of the court report. The letter of instruction should be detailed and spell out clearly what is required of the expert.

A good letter of instruction should include the following basic sections:

(a)   A statement in bold type of who is to be assessed; for example, the mother and/or the children, with dates of birth, where the court sits, the date by which the report is to be lodged at court, and who are the instructing parties.

(b)   A brief statement thanking the expert for agreeing to provide a report. It is helpful to point out here if there is any deadline for the lodging of the report, and a request to make clear at once if the deadline cannot be met. The letter should make clear here who is the lead solicitor and to whom the expert should address any queries.

(c)   The background to the current application and to the instructions.

This will include, for example, who are the parents and their children, when a referral was initially made to social services, and when care proceedings were first initiated and why. It will include a summary of any psychiatric history, including admissions to hospital, or where this information can be obtained in the accompanying bundle of papers. It will describe the more recent events leading up to the present proceedings, including a summary of any child protection meetings, interviews with professionals and any other experts already involved. The length of this section will obviously depend upon the nature of the problems and how long the family have been known to social services. The expert will greatly appreciate a good and even lengthy summary of the history at this point, as this will help them when they have to go through the documents in detail and try to make sense of what are often complex issues.

(d)   A summary of the proceedings and applications.

This may duplicate some of the background section, but it is useful to have the legal aspects of the case clearly described in chronological order. Thus, there may be a description of when an Emergency Protection Order was first taken out, when the first hearing of the local authority's application for an interim care order took place, when the case was transferred to a County Court, or higher, for reasons of complexity, and when directions were made and what they were.

Included in this section, or in a separate section, there should be a *summary of issues before the court*. For example this might be whether or not a mother should have an opportunity of undergoing a residential assessment, and if this should happen with one child or more than one child. The court may wish to know what should happen if the child were not to be returned to their family, and what alternative placements should be looked at in order to secure the child's best interests.

(e) A section on documents should either list what is enclosed or indicate where the list can be found in the enclosed bundle. There should be a statement that the expert can ask to see any further documents that they feel are necessary.

(f) The nature of the instructions.

It should be made clear, again on the nature of any joint instructions, that the expert is required to provide an independent opinion, and that all the parties need to be informed of discussions with any one party, along the lines already described above. The letter usually states that the expert may be required to attend a meeting with other experts in order to establish agreed facts and common findings, as well as areas of disagreement.

(g) The instructions.

These are usually laid out as a series of questions to be answered in the report. For example, the expert may be asked to comment on the mother's current mental health. If she has mental health problems the expert will be asked how, if at all, they impact on the mother's present and future ability to parent her child or children. There may be questions about a parent's treatability in general, and whether or not they were treatable in the child's time scale. That is, can the child wait for the parent to change. There may be issues concerning a parental couple; for example, whether or not there was any evidence of domestic violence and how this would affect the children. Questions may arise concerning any recommendations, such as whether or not the children require treatment, or should have alternative long-term carers, and, if so, recommendations for any future contact between parent and child. Finally, there is usually a question that asks the expert to give a view on any further investigation required, or any other issues not covered by the instructions that the expert thinks relevant.

(h) The expert will be reminded that in determining any question with respect to the child, they must adhere to the principle that the *child's welfare* is the court's paramount consideration.

The expert will also be reminded that the expert should express an opinion regarding the facts in the case, but they must not seek to resolve disputed facts, as this is the province of the judge. In addition, it may be stated that where appropriate it would be of assistance for the expert to express their opinion on the basis of alternative findings regarding the factual disputes—that is, to look at various alternative factual explanations and their clinical implications.

(i)   The letter of instructions usually ends with a summary of the proposed time scale and plan of work, and then a summary of how the fees are to be paid.

INTERPRETING THE PAPERS

First of all, it is important to look through the papers in order to make sense of the case and to see whether or not the instructions need modification at an early stage. It may not be necessary to look at everything in great detail, as is required before finally writing the court report, but there are certain essential elements that need to be examined.

The kind of things the expert needs to know, and which may determine whether or not it is worthwhile even to see the family for assessment, are as follows, and these are questions which are relevant if the family is seen subsequently.

(a)   Overall, the time factor dominates the considerations—the time the family have had the problems, the ages of the children and the need to get on with the decision making, the time it takes to get though the legal process, the time it may take to shift attitudes. Once the papers are received, one begins by looking for the referrer. One looks to see if there is a joint instruction, indicative of at least some kind of joint thinking, a willingness to get parties together to see what needs to be looked at. One cannot over-emphasize the importance of the parties cooperating; it would save so much professional and court time if this could happen at an early stage in sorting out a family assessment. Quite often the expert's only function when they finally arrive at court is to help parties think together, by providing a focus for their deliberations, something that could easily be done outside the court. Perhaps at such times the court is merely a place where at least people are forced to meet together, whether they like it or not.

Despite all the issues of funding a difficult family, which may or may not be disguised in the papers, and any doubts about a family's capacities, one looks in the papers for anyone who might hold out *hope* for a family. The fact that someone feels that they have formed a relationship with an otherwise difficult family may be important with regard to prognosis for change. The parents' lawyer may well be the only person to hold out hope for them. If the Guardian feels the same, then the expert can feel more confident about becoming involved in the case.

Next, the expert should look for the date of the final hearing that will make a decision about the child's future. There are occasions when an expert is asked to make an assessment a week before the final hearing, as a last ditch attempt to prevent adoption, despite all the assessments having been made by many other professionals. Needless to say, it is rare to agree to making such an assessment. There would really have to be an indication of gross injustice or incompetence to lead one to agree to disrupt the whole court process.

(b) Checking to see if all the *relevant documents* have been sent can be crucial. For example, I was recently sent two boxes of papers about a family who had already been extensively assessed by another colleague. I was asked to give my view, within a few days, about whether or not I would see the family. But the final report by my colleague, giving the detailed reasons why this family in his view were unable to look after their children, was not enclosed. In fact, once the report was finally received it became clear that it was not worth delaying the court process while yet another assessment was undertaken. This colleague had tried very hard to help the family over some months, but without much success. Of course, one might reasonably suspect that the late arrival of the report was intentional.

(c) The *history* provides the backdrop to the assessment, from which a picture of the family gradually emerges. The nature and extent of the family's problems, as well as any strengths, should become clear. With the multiple problem family, one must be wary of being too hardened about finding yet another story of childhood deprivation, abuse, a troubled adolescence, early pregnancies, children removed as a result of neglect or abuse, and troubled adult relationships with or without violence. Trying to keep an open mind about the story can be difficult. One should look for any signs of hope, such as some insight into the nature of the problems, a willingness to take responsibility for actions, some signs of a response to treatment, whether or not treatment has been offered, and if so what has happened. Because of the great variations in services throughout the country, what is on offer for a family may go from an occasional visit from a social worker to intensive work in a family centre. Thus, the quantity and quality of any previous work is relevant in judging what kind of assessment needs to be done, if any.

If possible one can begin to make a preliminary judgement about the parents' personalities and their capacity for change. Such a judgement may be different with a teenage single mother than with parents in their late twenties. One will expect less capacity to be independent with a teenager than with an adult, though professionals' anxiety about the teenager's ability to look after a baby is usually greater, even allowing for the fact that a teenager may be able to change fairly quickly.

Depth and quality of relationships with adults as well as with their children help to give a preliminary picture of personality. Those with a borderline personality may display turbulent relationships, moving from partner to partner, with lability of emotion, shifting between idealization and denigration of people, including professionals, frequent acting-out in self-destructive ways, and a general difficulty in making emotional contact with others, including their children.

It is common to find what one might call the *dynamics of deprivation*. This means that one can trace a pattern of relating with others, including professionals, which involves the parent unconsciously seeking an ideal mother, one who will always be there and who can provide twenty-four-hour care and concern. Though this is an understandable fantasy, given the fact that so many of the parents seen for assessment have had far from ideal upbringings, often with a long history of social and emotional deprivation, the fantasy itself is very destructive, for twenty-four-hour care can never be provided. Only a baby can receive such care, and the parent may become pregnant in order to obtain the care through their role as mother. They seek love from the baby rather than to give the baby their love. But this reverses the mother–baby relationship and often ends in frustration and anger, which may lead to the child being hurt or neglected because it cannot give back to the mother what she desires. Left with a terrible sense of emptiness inside, the deprived parent may then seek to find different ways of filling herself up. Common means for doing this include turning to food as comfort, to excitement from sex or drugs, or to attacking their bodies. The papers often reveal this kind of pattern of relating over years. A main aim of treatment is to help the individual come to terms with this unrealistic fantasy, so that they can begin to use the smaller amounts of help and care that can be available to them in an ordinary, ongoing way, rather than continue to pine for the impossible. This often involves the mother having to learn to love her baby.

(d)   Other necessary items of information from the papers may include medical reports, including those from the general practitioner and health visitor, the school reports, and the parents' own account of their situation.

(e)   Finally, the expert should try to get some picture of the professional network, which always reflects to some degree the family's own pathology. The degree of splitting between professionals may reflect the family's own difficulties in integrating experience. However, it can also be difficult to distinguish this kind of reflection of pathology from hardened positions taken up by different parties. Occasionally, a rigid position by one professional has even led to them being removed from the case. While the initial removal of the social worker in this kind of situation is rare, it does give an indication of the kind of difficult emotions that fly around in such work.

SUMMARY

The expert should be reluctant to see a multi-problem family for the first time just before a final hearing, or when they do not have the relevant documents, or when the parents take little or no responsibility for their actions.

They should usually agree when the parents show willingness to begin to reflect on their experience; that is, as will be described in detail below, to begin to examine their present and past behaviour and emotions, and to take some, however limited, responsibility for their actions. It is a good prognostic sign if the parents have shown some positive response to previous treatment interventions, and when the Guardian and at least one other feel that there is some hope, despite opposition from other parties.

The papers with single issue instructions, such as questions about contact, are usually straightforward. But the papers from multi-problem families require more study, and at times a judgement about whether or not it is worthwhile proceeding to a full assessment.

Once a decision is made to offer an assessment, then a certain mount of planning of what will happen is necessary, depending on the nature of the instructions. If there is a request for an assessment of a parent's personality and/or psychiatric state, all that needs to be planned is to set up a meeting with the parent. But with more complicated issues, involving the whole family, careful planning of what kind of meetings need to take place, and where they are to happen, may be necessary. For example, if a child has not been with the parents for some months, then a careful judgement about whether or not it is wise to see them all together will be necessary. It may be better to explore the issues with the parents first before proceeding to a whole family meeting. Observations from any contact visits may help the assessor decide how to proceed. For example, if the contacts have been regular, frequent, and without problems, then a whole family meeting may go ahead sooner rather than later; but if contacts have been full of conflict, then one may hesitate before arranging such a meeting.

Seeing the family

INITIAL IMPACT

Seeing the family in person can be a surprise. The papers may have built up a negative picture of a parent or a family, and yet when you actually meet them they do not seem that bad, and, indeed, may have some good points. Part of the assessment includes the initial impact a family makes on this first meeting. Of course, one still has to be aware of the history and the experience of other professionals, and the fact that the parents may be out to make a good impression and to belittle other workers. However, a desire to make a good impression is not in itself a bad thing, provided it is not accompanied by considerable denial of difficulties, for it may indicate a wish to be understood rather than condemned.

Making reasonably good emotional contact with the family, the parents and their children, is an essential part of the assessment process. It may or may not lead to a positive view of the parents' capacities, but lack of such contact is usually a bad prognostic sign, evidence of the parents' relating difficulties or their untreatability. What can be most difficult to judge, as already indicated, is the *convincingness* of the parents' account. For example, with a parent who made an admission of previous injuries to their child only at the outset of a court hearing, it is understandable that those who have dealt with the family for some months previously will be sceptical about the genuineness of the admission. The assessment may eventually turn around the degree to which the parent's remorse comes across as genuine, and that can be very difficult to gauge on the basis of one or two consultations. It may only become clear over a period of time and in a day or residential centre. A full admission of past actions may only be possible in the context of an ongoing therapeutic relationship. This highlights the point that the initial consultation may be merely the first stage in the assessment process; it may end up recommending a further and more extensive period of assessment elsewhere, when there is some hope of change but not enough evidence from the initial consultations that it is feasible.

Sometimes an admission of responsibility comes out from indirect techniques, such as asking the parents to imagine what their child felt like when he or she was abused, and then seeing how they respond; or asking them to put themselves back in time to when their child was crying too much or making excessive demands. Going back in time in this way may provoke memories of the abusing experience, when their child, for example, reminded them of their own abusive childhood.

Assessment interviews

WHO TO SEE?

A full assessment requires interviews with the parents and the children separately and together by one or more professionals. There are different approaches to how one goes about doing this. It is usual to see the family together for a little while, in order to get a feel for what they are like, to clarify what the children understand about why they are coming to see the expert, and to explain what they will be doing. One will then see the children and the parents separately, and possibly the whole family again at the end, either to explain views, or to observe them in more detail. Sometimes one see the parents on their own in detail on one occasion, and then the children at another time, either later that day or on another day, if the children have been separated from their parents for long periods and where there has been a major breakdown of the family's functioning. Putting the parents and children together in the same room when there have been major problems of abuse and when the children have been separated for some time, can be very difficult for the children, at least without some preliminary work.

With contact cases, seeing the family, and at what point to see the children, depends upon the nature of the issues the expert is asked to address. For example, in cases of domestic violence, one might initially offer appointments for the parents on separate days, before thinking of seeing them together, and one might not do that at all if there is a real risk of intimidation. However, in situations where there has essentially been a breakdown of communication, one might want to see the interaction of both parents, if they agree.

The core principles guiding decisions about contact issues have been well summarized by Sturge and Glaser (2000), and these will be examined in detail in subsequent chapters. In brief, they include making sure that decisions about contact are child-centred and can benefit the child. Maintaining contact with an absent parent can help the child's emotional growth and development, and can be an opportunity for reality testing for the child. It may help them feel less responsible for the breakdown of their parents' relationship, The benefit to the child has to be weighed against the risks of contact, direct or indirect. Such risks include that of being exposed to ongoing violence and intimidation, as well as the risk of being exposed to a parent with whom the child has no bond.

In addition, once continuing contact between parent and child has been recommended, there has to be a recommendation about the level of contact. Fundamentally, this will depend upon the reason for the contact. If the reason is to maintain the status quo, and to provide an opportunity to keep a link with an absent parent, then it might be regular but occasional contact. If the purpose is to change the situation, then the contact may be reduced or increased accordingly. If the plan is to move towards, for example, overnight stays, then contact should be increased. If the plan is to move towards adoption, then contact will be gradually reduced and even stopped, depending on whether or not there will be an open adoption. There might also be a recommendation about whether or not contact is to be supervised, depending upon the reliability of the absent parent, or the risks to the child of having unsupervised contact.

With the multi-problem family, one generally likes to see the whole family, not just the parents, in order to look at the quality of the relationships, so vital to making a proper assessment of what is best for the child. However, there are times when experts are not allowed by the court to do this, and just have to start with the parents, which of course gives only a limited view of the family and usually delays the whole decision-making process. There are a number of occasions, particularly when babies are involved, when there are persistent objections to the expert seeing the parents and children together, and where they may have to set out in detail why they think it is appropriate to do so. It can be really difficult to convince the local authority that a full assessment cannot take place without seeing the details of the parent–child relationship. It would be preferable for the court to allow the expert to make the clinical judgement about whether or not they see the children and at what point, rather than having to see the parents and then go back to court to ask permission to see the children, which entails considerable delay.

WHAT TO LOOK AT

When assessing the family, it is helpful to look at the family as a whole, or as a system, as well as looking at the individuals in their own right, including the parents' personalities, the attachment patterns of the children to their parents, and the inner worlds of the children. The clinical evidence for one's view comes from the history, the narrative of events provided by the family, and from observation of their ways of relating.

Looking at the family overall, one can observe how they deal with both everyday realities, such as eating, sleeping, getting the children to school, and how they cope with past and present traumatic situations.

The family's boundaries are particularly revealing of how they deal with any challenges both from within and without. Secure and flexible boundaries enable children to feel safe within the family and yet develop increasing independence from the parents. Muddled and constantly shifting boundaries make children feel insecure and confused about their development; they may be associated with intrusion into basic body boundaries, such as sexual abuse by a family member, with the most pernicious effect on the child's emotional development.

In the more disturbed families one may see various kinds of distorted family functioning, including excessive externalization of emotions; that is, the use of action rather than talking to deal with conflicts, as well as massive denial of responsibility for actions and emotions, accompanied by splitting and projection. The most obvious example of projection within the family is to blame one member of the family, the scapegoat, for all the family's difficulties. Alternatively, a family may blame all outsiders for their difficulties, projecting badness on to the outside rather than taking any personal responsibility for feeling bad. Overall, one is looking for the capacity of the family to contain anxieties without excessive projection; their ability to create a safe and good enough environment in which their children can develop from dependency to increasing independence, without risk of significant harm.

As well as a judgement about the family as a whole system, one looks at any young children's individual attachment patterns. There are four basic types of such patterns—*secure, avoidant, re-enacting,* and *disorganized.*

A *securely* attached child is able to deal with brief separations from their parent without excessive anxiety. On seeing the parent again, they respond by going up to the parent, and the latter reacts with affection and appropriate reassurance.

In the *avoidant* pattern, the children avoid contact when the parent tries to get close; it is often associated with parents who are highly ambivalent towards, and rejecting of, their children.

The *re-enacting* pattern is seen with parents who see only negative aspects in their children's behaviour, with excessive punishment being used to deal with any so-called "difficult" behaviour. The parents may be either intrusive or rejecting, and the children are in turn ambivalent about being close to the parent, showing either rejection or excessive clinging on returning to the parent after a brief period of separation. Typically, role reversal is obvious, with the child acting as parent to the mother or father.

With *disorganized* attachments, the children show confused and highly anxious responses on their return after periods of separation from their parents. The latter show marked difficulties in keeping their children in mind, and react to them with a variety of rejecting and confused responses. Many of the children in multi-problem families have such disorganized attachment patterns; for example, on getting close to their mother they may show various kinds of confusional states. It can be helpful for these children to be exposed in treatment settings to a sequence of more stable and organized attachments. One can then gradually help to build up trust between the parent and child in order to increase the sense of security between them.

HOW TO DO IT

When interviewing children the following scheme can be used, which can be adapted to the age of the child:

Initially, one aims to make the child feel at ease, perhaps by asking them a little about themselves, such as what they play, what kinds of games they like, and what they watch on television. Then one turns to school issues, unless the main problem is there.

The interviewer can ask them about what subjects they like and then what they do not like, eliciting some details of what they might be doing in class, what stories, if any, they have written, what topics in other subjects they are currently involved with. One asks if they have a close friend or just lots of friends. The isolated child tends to say they have many friends. One is trying try to build up a picture of their relationships with the teachers and the other pupils, and how they feel about their school, before moving on to the home situation, which may be the most fraught area for them.

Younger children will play with some toys, such as small dolls, pens and paper, a telephone, a tea set, some cars, or a teddy bear. It may be necessary to play with the child in order to put them at ease, but also to elicit information. Very young children can really only communicate through play, and so one does not expect them to give a coherent story about their lives. Instead, the interviewer will need to comment on the play and make the occasional interpretation of it. For example, if a child takes hold of the parent dolls and makes the father and mother fight a lot, then one can obviously comment on what they are doing, and then gently ease towards wondering if their own parents fight in front of them. Interpreting the significance of child play requires experience; there needs to be an awareness of the developmental level of the child, their age and maturity. From about the age of five onwards, the interviewer can use a mixture of play and direct questioning to build up a picture of the child's inner world, moving from one to the other as the interview progresses.

When tackling the home situation, one asks the child about their parents, if they can describe them at all, if they are kind or strict, angry or calm, etc. This may be difficult for younger children, especially if they are defensive about their parents. Older children may be able to answer a direct question about how they would describe their parents, but it may be easier to ask them how their parents would respond to a particular situation, for example if the child did something such as make a mess or answer back. One might then begin to build up a picture of parental attitudes.

If there are siblings, one can ask similar questions, and then enquire about where the children sleep, and how they get on with one another as well as with their parents. One should also ask about any extended family and their involvement. By this time, the family problems may well be in focus, for example if there is excessive violence, or sexual abuse, or the presence of an ill parent, or if the child stays at home and refuses to go to school.

Having, one hopes, built up trust with the child, the interviewer will then directly tackle whatever is the main area of anxiety, or the main problem, asking specific questions if necessary, depending on the age of the child, in order to elicit information about what happened and how they were affected. This part of the interview is often the most difficult but also the most revealing, and requires patience; the child cannot be hurried.

Having reached the main difficulties, one should begin to wind down the interview, with the aim of letting the child leave the room without excessive anxiety. There are usually a few specific questions one will want answered at some point and which can be slipped in, such as whether or not the child goes through rituals and obsessions, or has nightmares, or suffers from specific phobias or somatic symptoms. One can also ask them to make three wishes, as a way of entering into their fantasy world. The interviewer should also give them the opportunity to ask any question; and it can be useful, towards the end, to ask them to draw a picture, if they have not already done so.

The latter activity can help them get themselves together by the end of the interview, so that they return to their parent in a reasonably calm state. Thus, the whole interview, ideally, has a certain shape—a gradually rising tension, followed by winding down and release. Ideally, by the end the child feels they have been understood.

Seeing the family together requires somewhat different skills than those needed with the individual child. One attempts to look at the family as a whole rather than as a collection of individuals. While there will be specific questions to be addressed with the family about the history and how they currently function, there is a more specific focus on their overall interaction. One will look at how the parents interact with the children, whether or not they can listen to them or just talk over them, how much they can keep the children in mind. There will be attention to how the couple function, whether or not they can listen to each other, how much they support one another, how much their preoccupations take precedence over the children's needs. It is useful to ask specific questions about how the family members deal with everyday tasks, such as eating together, in order to obtain a clear picture of how the parents can cope with the children. Chaotic families may not be able to do the simplest tasks without major problems. How the family deal with the reality of the interview situation is itself a vital part of the assessment, in that those who are reluctant to think about the children with the interviewer are unlikely to be able to do so in the outside world. A family without clear boundaries in the interviewer's consulting room, where the children are neglected and left to fight among themselves, is likely to have major problems in their own home. Obviously the papers may confirm whether or not this is the case.

An important part of the interviewing process is how the parents and the children respond to the interviewer's interventions. The latter vary greatly, depending upon the interviewer's approach; how much, for example, they focus on the family dynamics, or on the individuals making up the family, how much they enter into the child's inner world or remain observers of the child's behaviour. One can look at how the members of the family, both together and separately, respond to interpretations, which is fundamental to any understanding of both family dynamics and the individual's capacity for self reflection and for change. For example, one will look for underlying anxieties, the defences against anxiety, and any guilt about wishes and desires, as well as any insight into the connections between past and present behaviour. One can make simple comments such as "That must make you feel anxious", or "I notice you felt worried talking about that", leading up to a more formal interpretation, such as "I wonder if you have ever connected your violent relationships with men to the way your father treated you and your mother". Seeing connections between past and present realities, and a curiosity about these connections, is a hopeful sign, indicative of some capacity for self reflection.

Alternatively, one can focus on the family as a system, only making comments about how the whole family interact, such as comments about there being no place for a child in this family, or that the couple's own conflictual relationship dominates the family so much that there is no space for the children, who have to be violent in order to get any attention.

My personal preference is for a mixed approach, where there is attention both to the individual members of the family and to the family as a whole system. That way, there is less risk of missing something important both with the individual child and with the family.

NETWORK MEETINGS

Doing assessments that do not involve the courts often requires meeting various workers either before or after having seen the family, in order to get some insight on the way a family deals with outside relationships, and this can be very useful as a guide to how the family functions as well as how the professionals are coping with the family. Such meetings with families who are involved with the court can be equally enlightening, although they also tend to provoke more anxiety in professionals, because the issues involved are often starker. For example, if decisions have to made about whether or not a baby should remain with a mother who has caused it serious injuries, it is natural that workers want to be convinced that any plan that involves keeping them together does not lead to further injuries. Ideally, a network meeting should offer the chance to think about the issues involved in an open-minded way, though it may also be an occasion where hardened and inflexible positions are maintained, reflecting not only workers' anxiety but also splits within the family itself. Coming into the latter kind of meeting can be very uncomfortable; chairing such a meeting requires considerable patience and a great capacity for biting one's tongue. The meeting needs to allow workers to have their say, and then see if it is possible to find a common language to describe the issues.

While social workers often will be mainly concerned with child protection issues and can find it difficult to see the meaning behind behaviour, mental health professionals will tend to see these underlying meanings and be more alert to possible change. Both positions have their importance, and neither should be ignored.

For example, some workers were rightly worried about a couple who had severely injured a previous child and then had a new baby. For various reasons, the couple still had daily access to the new baby, despite the fact that social services wished to have the baby adopted. In fact, the previous child had been injured a number of years previously, and the couple's attitude had shifted somewhat by the time they finally had a new baby. But the workers in the meeting clearly found it difficult to adjust to the new reality, with all their memories of what had happened in the past still dominating them; they found it difficult to understand that the reason the courts had delayed any decision about adoption was that a full assessment of the new situation had not been undertaken, partly because social services kept asserting that the family had already been assessed years before, and that nothing had changed. The workers were right to keep their child protection worries in the foreground, but wrong in maintaining a fixed attitude to the parents' new situation. It required a long and often tense meeting to hammer these issues out, and to obtain agreement to allow the parents a full assessment, without the necessity of asking the court to order it. The workers were allowed to retain their scepticism about the outcome of the assessment, and we were allowed to retain our slightly more positive view of the parents' capacities.

Main criteria for assessing parenting

In order to bring together in a report the various observations about the family, it can be helpful to have some kind of formalized scheme or set of questions which have to be addressed. One should make clear that one is not looking for the perfect parent, but only for the *reasonably good enough* parent, given the family's difficult circumstances. It is likely that one will detect a number of problems, but the issue is how severe they are and whether or not they are capable of being treated.

The *first* criterion, already referred to above, concerns the degree to which a parent can take responsibility for their actions, which often in these circumstances, involves owning up to past abuse of their children. It may not be possible to discover all the details of what took place; this may never happen, or many details may only come to light if the parent is in a therapeutic relationship that can gradually uncover what has been denied and repressed. But without some basic willingness to admit past harmful actions, a family is untreatable.

In addition, what is significant for an assessment of treatability is not just an admission of past actions, but an admission *with appropriate affect*. Thus, for example, a mother who had injured her young baby soon admitted to her actions once the child had been diagnosed in casualty. She continued to admit what she had done, but there was a worrying quality to how she did so. She would easily come out with the words about her actions, and even produce tears, but there was an absence of convincing feelings accompanying the words. Beneath her veneer of a capable person, she was full of seething resentments. For example, her own mother had left the family home when she was young, leaving her to become the "little mother" to her siblings. She bore all this with apparent equanimity, but in therapy it became clear how resentful she was underneath. She had then succeeded in work, quickly gaining promotion and being responsible for those older than herself. She had enormous pride in being so capable. But when her baby was born, she could not cope with the crying and the baby's neediness. She unconsciously resented the fact that the baby made her feel helpless, but to admit openly such feelings of helplessness in herself was very difficult, because it went against her whole picture of herself as coping and efficient. The words with which she described what she had done to the baby continued to sound rehearsed and hollow; it was only after some weeks of treatment, which challenged her fixed view of herself and her capacities, that the façade began to crack, and she began to sound real for the first time.

Making a clinical judgement about whether or not it is worthwhile to offer a parent a chance to make such shifts can be very difficult. One hopes that initially the parent has a basic understanding of past events, with a certain amount of detail available, and that they are willing to seek help and can make some positive response to comments about themselves. To have a *successful outcome*, parents need to acknowledge that there were problems within the family, that the problems were in the main of their own making, and that they needed help. But a common complicating factor for these families in the adversarial legal system to which they are exposed is that the parents may feel that admission of failure, including harming a child, may be used against them in court proceedings. Gaining the family's trust in order to reassure them that admissions of failure are in their interest can be quite tricky, particularly for social workers, who have statutory responsibilities. It may be easier for a mental health worker to establish an effective alliance, as they are a little apart from the legal processes.

The *second* main criterion for assessing parental capacity is the adequate provision of physical care, including being physically present for the child, providing for their physical needs, such as food, drink, warmth, a place to live, appropriate clothing, and adequate hygiene. This is fairly easy to assess, from a home visit, and from pooling information from other workers. Providing adequate physical care is obviously most crucial with babies, as failures quickly produce crises. But it is often the case that, even with highly problematic families, the basic physical care of the babies is adequate.

Problems usually lie elsewhere, such as with a baby in the emotional bonding, or with other children in the relationships between parent and child. While one must make allowances for poverty and poor housing, a global inability to provide basic physical care is often associated with poor parenting capacity.

However, most multi-problem families have some kind of difficulty in attending to some aspects of basic physical care throughout the day, a problem with what one could call the "work of the day" (Kennedy, 1987), which usually provides the structure for everyday life. The work of the day is focused around essential activities such as eating, sleeping, and working. Such events, ritualized and structured to a varied extent, provide the emotional context that drives practical life. Normally one performs the day's activities without thinking about their basic structure. With the families under consideration, however, the things that most people do without thinking, or do even with a lot of hard work, are charged with conflict, so that there is a breakdown in the continuity and consistency of daily life, leading to the family's inability to attend appropriately to the ordinary everyday tasks of living, at least in some areas.

Criterion *three* refers to consistency of behaviour and functioning with regard to the child, and includes providing appropriate and safe boundaries, respecting the child's own world, perceiving the child as different from the adult and with different needs, and providing appropriate restraint of adult needs and impulses. The parent should be able to provide some kind of model of appropriate social behaviour, so that the child can learn to mix with others satisfactorily.

The nature of the parental relationship is relevant in judging what model they offer to their children. Domestic violence and extreme marital conflict are obviously extremely detrimental to the children's welfare.

A difficulty in boundary keeping and effective and safe disciplining is a common complaint in problem families. It is also one of the most frequent causes for professional concern. For example, a common anxiety around assessing a parent with a baby is what will happen when the baby becomes more independent and testing of the parent.

While a parent may be good when the child is very dependent, and, indeed may have become pregnant in order to re-experience the powerful feeling of having a helpless baby to look after, the parent may have had great difficulties with previous children when they started to walk and began to assert their independence from the parent. Professionals often object to treating a problem family with a baby because it can be difficult to predict how the parent will cope with more challenging behaviour. Thus, while one may have a reasonably positive view of the family's ability to look after a baby, there is always a degree of uncertainty about how they will respond to a toddler; and embarking on a prolonged course of treatment to encompass the later developmental stages will delay decision-making about the child's future.

There are no easy answers to these kinds of doubts about embarking on family treatment, except to be mindful of them. One could add that it is important to look at the whole clinical picture of the family, not just one aspect of their functioning. While the family's ability to provide safe boundaries may be in question because of the history, they may show other more positive aspects of functioning in the here-and-now.

The *fourth* criterion—the capacity to empathize with the child, including, for example, how the parents respond to a child's emotional and physical pain, whether or not they express love and concern or rejection and hatred, and the degree of any ambivalence—is crucial in assessing a parent's ability to understand the impact of their own behaviour on the child's well-being.

With mothers and babies, one is particularly looking at the developing bond between them, which can be difficult to judge, particularly if the baby is placed in foster care at an early age. That is, assessing a bond when the parent has only had contact visits rather than the full-time care of the baby can be difficult. A very negative early relationship may be obvious, with the parent unable to care physically or emotionally in the contact sessions, and the baby looking unhappy, crying and struggling because of the unempathic parental responses. But more frequently there are no particularly bad observations; the baby may be happy to see the parent, but also not too bothered when they are returned to the foster parent, and the parents do what they can to make the child enjoy the contact.

Empathy in this context involves a capacity to put oneself in the child's shoes, to try to feel what they are feeling, as opposed to imposing what the parent feels on the child, or not allowing the child to have any sense of being separate from the parents. Along with empathy one would expect appropriate close physical contact and expressions of warmth. An ability to give praise is particularly positive, as so many of the problem families have difficulty in doing this. One so often sees a vicious circle of negative behaviour in the child and negative feedback from the parent. One usually has to form a judgement about the degree of negativity and the parents' capacity to respond to interventions to cut through the vicious negative circle. Thus, it would be a good prognostic sign if a parent can listen to a comment about offering more praise for good behaviour rather than always responding to the negative.

How the parent *talks* to the child is relevant here, whether or not they can communicate at the child's level, and whether or not they can anticipate difficulties on behalf of the child. A capacity for *play* may be an important indicator of a reasonable child–parent relationship, even when several other indicators are negative. Such a capacity indicates sufficient trust and intimacy between parent and child. Woodenness in play, or very confused play, may be indicative of poor parenting, especially when combined with one or more of the other parenting criteria. There are, however, circumstances when a parent is good at playing but still cannot provide a safe enough environment for the child. This is when the parent likes being a child themselves, enjoys the intensity of child-like interactions, but has great difficulties in also maintaining adult responsibilities.

The *fifth* criterion—the degree of a capacity for trust—reflects the quality of the relationships, both within the family and between the family and the professionals. Trust implies secure attachments, and thus a clear picture of insufficient trust is an indicator of attachment difficulties. An ability to use professionals appropriately is often a good prognostic sign, indicative of some trusting capacities.

Placement issues may come into the picture; for example, if a child is in foster care one will assess the quality of the parents' contact visits. This can be done by reading observations from any contact supervisors, but a judgement also needs to be made about whether or not the assessor needs to see a contact visit for themselves, and, occasionally, this is specifically requested in the instructions.

The assessor needs to look at the ability of the parent to provide a trusting atmosphere for their children, at home or during contacts. For example, it is usually a sign of poor parenting if the family belief system maintains that all outsiders are bad and to be avoided, that the world, including school, is a dangerous place and so is not be explored. Such families often come across as strange, as they maintain bizarre beliefs about themselves and their surroundings.

A more usual pattern of parenting is one where dependency for young children is encouraged, yet increasing independence from the parents and the home is also gradually encouraged, allowing the children to grow into autonomous adults. That is, one is looking for some flexibility and adaptability within the family system.

Dealing with *adolescent* children requires some ability to negotiate, to provide consistency and a degree of firmness, but at the same time a willingness to listen to the adolescent's point of view and open negotiations.

The *sixth* criterion includes other factors such as a judgement about a capacity for change and the role of the history.

Judging a family's capacity for change involves looking at the various elements of parenting, and seeing how much the parents demonstrate some capacity for insight into their problems and a shift in the quality of their relationships. The initial stage of the assessment may entail making some kind of description of the family system and each individual's wishes, needs, and difficulties, but then it is important to move into seeing how much shift in the family is possible. It may well be that it is only the children who show any capacity for change, with the parents resisting the impact of their children's ability to shift. If the parents in a highly disordered family cannot change, then one may end up recommending permanent removal of the children.

Historical factors come into the picture, both at the beginning of the assessment, as the backdrop for the interviews, but also throughout the assessment. Many parents who have difficulty taking on parental responsibility have had deprived childhoods, and a number of them have been physically and/or sexually abused as children. Never having being allowed to be ordinary children themselves, some of these abused adults are compelled to harm their children. But historical factors in themselves may only indicate risk factors. Not all abusing parents were abused as children, though the great majority have had emotionally deprived upbringings.

The history will also be important when making a diagnosis of the parents' personalities and any psychiatric condition. Most of the parents have some kind of personality difficulties but they do not necessarily hang together into a formal diagnostic category. They often have deprived histories, a stormy adolescent period and relatively unstable relationships, with difficulties in establishing a secure sense of their own identity. Periods of depression are common, particularly after the birth of a baby. Occasionally it is possible to make a formal diagnosis, such as mood disorder or borderline personality, but one still has to assess how this may impact on their parenting capacities. One may end up giving descriptive statements referring to, for example, the parent's fragility, their difficulty in maintaining a stable lifestyle, or their difficulty keeping the child in mind for long as they are so occupied by their own problems, rather than making much of a formal psychiatric diagnosis.

Putting it all together

Putting together all the information available and elicited, and making sense of it, is a complex task. The different elements of the assessment do not necessarily come together in a neat fashion. The letter of instructions is often helpful in focusing on questions that need to be addressed. In general, there are certain basic issues that the assessment needs to have covered. Fact finding is important in clarifying the nature of the problem presented. This will include making a clinical judgement about the dynamics of the family, how they interact with each other and with the professional network, as well as the degree to which the children are suffering from *significant harm*, whether from emotional, physical or sexual abuse, or all three forms of abuse.

Emotional abuse can be difficult to be precise about. It usually refers to the inability of the parent to respond adequately to the child's needs, so that the child's development is seriously impaired. One needs to be able to link the parental failure to the child's symptoms or complaints; for example, if a child shows behavioural and emotional difficulties in a home where basic physical care is lacking, or if a parent refuses to allow a child to go to school because they themselves cannot allow the child to leave them, and the child subsequently develops anxiety attacks. One may see various kinds of child–parent relationships, such as an over-close relationship between parent and child, which stifles the child's development, as in the typical school refusing situation, or else a rejecting and distant relationship that leaves the child as deprived as the parent themselves.

Assessing the degree of risk to the child includes looking at their overall emotional welfare, including the ability of the parent to put the child's needs first, as well as the degree to which the child may be physically at risk, for example in a home where domestic violence occurs.

Clearly, overall one is making a judgement about reasonably good enough parenting, what is expected of a parent in relation to the developmental needs of their children, as well as the circumstances that have led to a family being in trouble. Having defined the problem and some of the possible causal factors, one also looks for some capacity for sustainable change. While it may be possible to have a view about the likelihood of change, it may only be possible to have a firm view about this after the family have had a longer period of assessment in a clinic, day unit or, occasionally, in a residential setting. Because one is often making life-changing decisions about a child's future, it is important to have as much information as possible about any capacity for change, so that a judgement can be made about the advantages and disadvantages of pursuing treatment. The assessment can be very helpful in providing the framework for subsequent work with the family, and for this reason it is useful for the assessor to put in their report various possible treatment interventions, and a plan of action for the family, depending upon the outcome of the court case.

Writing the report

While there is no standard way of producing the court report, there are various guides to what needs to be put in the report and how it can be done, such as Black, Harris-Hendricks, and Wolkind (1998), the Expert Witness Pack produced by the Official Solicitor, and Wall (2000). There is a checklist of what the court needs to address in care proceedings and opposed private law applications. The court must take account of the ascertainable wishes and feelings of the child, in the light of their age and understanding, the child's physical, emotional, and educational needs, the likely effect of any change in circumstances, the child's age, sex, and cultural background, any significant harm the child has suffered, and the capacity of the parents, or any other relevant person, to meet the child's needs. The court will only make an order defining what is to happen to the child if it is better for the child to do so than not to do so. The judge has to be convinced that is in the child's best interest to make an order.

Wall (2000, p. 49) states that the court looks above all for clarity in the presentation of the report and in the conclusions reached, and that the court is concerned with:

(1)   the issues it asked you to address;
(2)   the material you have considered;
(3)   the conclusions you have reached; and
(4)   your reasons for reaching those conclusions.

It is important to have in mind the fact that whatever is put into the report will be scrutinized in detail by lawyers, who are expert at looking at the details of what words may mean, and that you may well have to stand up in court to justify your views.

Although this can be a daunting experience, as I have described in the introduction, it is some comfort to keep in mind that you are looked upon as an expert, and that you have expertise and experience that the court usually appreciates and needs in order to make a decision about a child's future life.

It is difficult to give guidance about how and when to do the report, as clinicians vary in the way they work. I usually leave at least a day before dictating the report, so that my views about the family have had time to crystallize. Sometimes it is obvious what to recommend, but at other times the situation is so complex that one needs time for thoughts to come together, and even then it may only be after the main report has been dictated that the recommendations become clear. That is, the act of putting together the report can be clarifying in itself. Obviously, it is best not to wait too long before dictating the report, as the freshness of the contact with the family may be lost, and the various details from the documents harder to remember.

The following is an outline of what a court report should contain, based on my experience and the above references:

PRESENTATION

Guidelines for the report's layout include:

- large typeface;
- numbered paragraphs;
- double spacing, A4 sheets with numbered pages, short sentences and paragraphs;
- clear English, avoiding too much jargon;
- separate sections for the assessment, the opinion and any recommendations;
- ideally, less than twenty pages where possible;
- table of contents if more than eight pages;
- details of interviews and documents seen, either in the main report or in an appendix.

STRUCTURE AND CONTENT

The first page of the report should include:

- the nature of the proceedings and the court reference number;
- the title of the document and the date of its origination;
- the subject's name, date of birth, and status;
- the author's name, qualifications, address, phone number and, if wished, e-mail address.

Having provided basic information about the case and the expert, the expert may well prefer to start the report proper by giving a brief summary of their view about what should happen before giving the clinical evidence for that view. That way, those reading the report do not have to wade through many pages before finding out what the expert essentially thinks. Thus, one might start by stating what one has been asked to do, and then the outcome of the assessment. For example, one might say that one has been asked to assess whether or not a child should remain with their parents, and that as a result of seeing the family and reading through the various reports, one considers that it would be in the best interests of the child to remain with their parents at the moment, but that the parents needed ongoing assessment over some weeks in order to establish some certainty about their commitment to change. Or, that in the expert's view, the father should have regular but supervised access to his children, etc.

One should then explain what will follow in the report and in what order.

Introductory information should include the following:

- The author's CV, with their experience relevant to the case and the issues to be addressed. Only a paragraph is required, not several pages with all their publications. However, there are a number of occasions when a full CV is requested by lawyers before the expert is instructed, so it is useful to keep one regularly updated.
- Identification of the report as one written for the party instructing the author, or as a joint instruction, giving a summary of reasons for making the report.
- Reference to the letter of instructions. One can either list the questions to be addressed at this point, or, in order to save space, leave them until they are answered in detail later in the report, but one needs explain that is what is to be done.
- A synopsis of sources of information, with a list of what has been given to the expert, if necessary in an appendix.

Background information should be set out with:

- a summary of the facts, including the history of the case, from reports and informants, and sources of information;
- hypotheses guiding the assessment, where possible.

The assessment proper should include:

- Interviews, clinical facts about the child, parents, other carers including foster carers, family, etc. Experts vary in their opinion as to how much description of the interviews should be put into the report. The advantage of describing what happened in detail is that it makes clear to the court the clinical evidence on which any opinion is based. The disadvantage is that it can be difficult to read through what might be several pages of clinical description, including interactions between the family members as well as between the family and the expert. The expert has to judge what makes most sense in a particular case; sometimes it is better to put more detailed description in an appendix, leaving an overall account of interviews in the main report.

- Clinical facts obtained through other investigations, such as videotaped interviews, or other assessments.
- Summary of main findings from the interviews, emphasizing where possible how any inferences are based upon clinical facts found.

The expert's opinion comes next, and needs to deal with the following, as appropriate:

- Overall nature of the issues and a clinical formulation of the family's situation.
- General diagnostic conclusions about the child and family. In fact, a formal diagnosis of the child and/or parents is often either not possible or not particularly relevant. However, what is often most relevant is a clear clinical formulation of the problems, including any risks to the child.

A summary, with evidence, of any formal child abuse is vital.

- Psychiatric/psychological diagnosis of the child, where possible.
- Psychiatric/psychological diagnosis of the parents or carers, where possible.
- Identification of resources necessary to meet the child's needs
- Comment, where appropriate, on what legal orders might be beneficial to the child.
- Answers to questions posed in the letter of instruction.

At this point, one should go through the questions asked of the expert in turn, even though this may well mean repeating what has already been stated in the report. It is useful for the court to have the expert's views encapsulated in these questions, as the court works by asking questions of witnesses. It may not be possible to answer all the questions, as they may vary in their relevance to the case. Where the expert cannot answer, they should say so and why. The answers should be as concise and to the point as possible, referring where necessary to the main body of the report for more clinical evidence.

The report should end with the expert's recommendations. While this may mean more repetition, it is still important to put all one's views together at this point, and go though the various options available, briefly explaining the pros and cons of each one. For example, there may be an issue of removal of a child from the family and a recommendation for adoption. One should not just recommend removal, but also look at other options, with a comment about the advisability of following them, including the benefits to the child of, say, remaining with the parents. It is most helpful to the court if a clear final recommendation is provided. However, there are occasions when this is not advisable, and the expert needs to explain why this is the case. It may only be possible to put forward various alternative recommendations, with the risks attached to each. It will, of course, then be up to the court to decide which recommendation is to be followed.

The rules of court require that a statement is put in at the end of the report as follows:

> I declare that this statement is true to the best of my knowledge and belief, and I understand that it may be placed before the Court.
>
> Signed: _____ Dated:_____

The request for the fee, which should have been negotiated at the beginning of the expert's involvement, is sent out with the report.

Meetings of experts

Once the report is written, it is sent to the lead solicitor, who then sends copies out to various parties. Nothing much may happen for some time, depending on the report's recommendations, whether or not the parties agree with the expert's views, and what may have happened to the family in the meantime.

When there are other experts involved in the case, a meeting between them can be very useful in clarifying issues, and may well have been ordered by the court to take place within a given time scale. As Wall (2000) states:

> Meetings of experts pursuant to a direction from the court are an important forensic item. They can save much time, by narrowing issues or by reaching agreement, thereby rendering the oral evidence of experts unnecessary. However, a strict intellectual discipline must be applied to them. Whilst the logistics of setting up, conducting and reporting on such meetings are largely matters for the lawyers, experts have a vital role in ensuring that meetings are set up only when they are necessary and that they are productive. [Wall, 2000, p. 35]

The Children's Guardian, or their lawyer, is often responsible for the difficult task of arranging the experts' meeting, and for taking the minutes. Sometimes it is only possible to have a teleconference, which is perfectly acceptable.

It is helpful to have a list of questions pre-circulated, so that the experts can have time to consider their views, thus saving time taken up by the actual meeting. Questions to be asked might be, for example, about:

- time scales for any intervention;
- whether or not a parent can make changes rapidly enough and within the child's time scales;
- whether or not there is agreement on fundamental points;
- where there are disagreements, what they are and on what basis the differing views are put forward;
- details of options recommended by each party, with agreements and disagreements;
- a summary of any overall agreement and a clear statement of differing views.

It is usual to ask the various parties to look at the minutes afterwards and to correct any mistakes or misrepresentations, and then to sign them as correct. It may well be that one or more expert changes their view once the meeting has taken place. The reasons for this should be made plain at the meeting or, if necessary, subsequently. Changing one's view is perfectly acceptable, particularly where there is fresh information about the family, so long as there are clear reasons given for so doing.

CHAPTER THREE

The "best worst option": three examples

I t is rare to come away from a family assessment thinking that one has recommended an easy option. Decisions about a child's future have to be made, and that usually means that someone is going to suffer, including the child. If a child is going to be reunited with their parents, then they will lose valuable foster parents; if the decision is to remove children from harmful parents, the children will still miss their parents, and will usually try to make contact with them when they become adolescent, however abusive they may have been. Siblings may have to be separated, one parent may lose the right for any direct contact, families in treatment will have to face difficult thoughts and feelings, a child placed with adopted parents may be abused by them. Hence the title of this chapter; there is no perfect answer in this work; there is no certainty. The examples given, taken from my own case-load, try to show something of the complexity of the issues that are addressed in the detail of these kinds of situation. While in each case clear recommendations came out of the assessment process, it took some time to reach them and there were no easy answers.

The first example

Background

This concerns a mother, stepfather, and three children, an older boy aged four from the mother's previous relationship, and two younger children, girls aged two years and nine months, respectively, from the current relationship. All three children were removed into care a few months prior to the assessment because of long-standing emotional harm. The older boy had a history of difficult behavioural and educational problems; the parents had great difficulty in providing firm boundaries, neglected his physical care, and seemed unable to work effectively with their social service department. The younger children were less of a handful, but workers commented on the general difficulties the parents had in providing consistent care for them, as well as an inability to attend to their emotional needs. There were suggestions that the older girl had some behavioural problems, and the label "Attention deficit disorder", which involves a child being hyperactive, unable to concentrate, and with behavioural problems, had crept into one report about her.

Instructions

In the first place I was asked by her solicitor to assess the mother with regard to her parenting qualities in the light of the fact that her children had been removed into foster care because of emotional abuse and neglect. The reason I was called in was that an assessment by a family organization had concluded that the children should not remain with the parents. Initially, I was asked to examine the report from this organization, and because I thought the conclusions were somewhat doubtful, I considered it worth going ahead with my own assessment. However, I was not allowed to see the children at first, and had to rely on the observations of the other professionals. What was in dispute were the conclusions from the observations, since I considered that these were parents who needed a comprehensive package of intervention—something the family had never had—before considering removal of at least the younger children, Unfortunately, this is a situation I have frequently encountered over the years—extensive assessments may be made, but little attempt to see how a family can change, and problem families are not offered a clear strategy of therapeutic work at the intensive level they need.

First interview

I had only a limited view of the situation, as a result of one interview with the mother and reading through the many documents, but I felt that the decision about removal of the younger children needed to be reviewed, although I thought, along with the other professionals, that the four-year-old boy was so disturbed that clearly he needed to be placed outside the family, even though it would mean being removed from day-to-day contact with his siblings. I also considered that his removal would also probably make it easier for the parents to deal more effectively with the younger children.

The interview with the mother was fairly straightforward, in that she was pleasant, cooperative, and willing to talk about herself and her situation as best she could, though with limited understanding of the emotional aspects of her and her family's situation. She agreed that she had difficulties, but she repeatedly told me that she had asked for help but had never received any. However, I could see that it might be difficult for people, particularly those with relatively limited experience, to be able to find a way of offering her suitable help, as she tended to minimize the seriousness of her difficulties. She had welcomed help in the past from a family aide worker, from neighbours and friends, and the occasional professional when they had been very clearly supportive; she did not welcome being confronted with difficulties. In fact, the documents revealed that there was a time when the boy was very young when she did respond well to help and when her day-to-day routines were beginning to improve, but this period was short-lived, as was the help offered.

She told me that she lived with her partner, the father of the two younger children, but all the children had been removed into care three months previously. They had regular contact at a family centre. I wondered how the contact visits went. She said that on the one hand the children were happy to see them; however, they were asking why they couldn't come home, and she and her partner knew they could not say when this would be, and this meant that both the parents and the children were distressed when they had to separate. She did not seem to have much of a clue about how to make the partings more manageable, but neither had she been given any help to do so. She described playing with the children during the contact visits, and having no difficulty with them at that time. However, we went into the main difficulties she had with the older boy. These were connected with long-standing behavioural problems, for which she said she had repeatedly asked for help. He had been on the waiting list for eighteen months for help, and when finally they received help from a psychologist this did make a difference, but then it was stopped. The boy would not listen or do what he was told, and her partner found it difficult coping with him, particularly as he was not his father. The older girl had been rubbing herself with a cushion and they were both worried about this and asked for help, although she does not do it now. She felt she had no problems with the baby, however.

What came across throughout the interview was how much the mother minimized difficulties, and found it difficult to recognize emotional issues. However, she did agree that she needed help, and gradually demonstrated some grudging acceptance that some of the difficulties were linked to her own family background.

Family background

She had not talked to her family for some time. She was in a children's home as a teenager because her father was accused of sexually abusing her and her sisters; unfortunately she was not kept with her sisters, for reasons she could not recall. The father was imprisoned for the abuse, and her mother was also sentenced for being part of the situation. She described her father as horrible, physically violent to the children and her mother. In fact, he was back with her mother, whom she found it difficult to describe as a person. However, the mother showed more affection than the father. She could not recall much of her early childhood, but she recalled how difficult school became when the abuse became public.

She became pregnant when she was eighteen by a boyfriend with whom she had a stormy relationship, though he never beat her. Social services became involved as they had difficulties in coping as a family, but her son was not removed.

We covered her more recent relationship, and how she had been coping with her daughters and her son and the difficulties he created for the whole family. She became involved with her new partner soon after her first one left, and she had also lost the support of a health visitor and a family aide, giving the picture of a needy and dependent person, unable to fend for herself.

Overall picture of mother

It was clearly difficult to get a full picture of what was going in from this one meeting, particularly as the mother had limited emotional understanding with regard to the needs of the children. Clearly her own disturbed background had left her with these difficulties.

Psychological testing, which had been instigated because she seemed rather slow in understanding, had not shown any learning difficulties; instead she had problems in learning about emotions. Being out of touch with the children had led to her putting them in situations of emotional risk; for example, not protecting the younger children from the aggression of her son.

A family organization had done a full report on the parents and the children. Their observations of the mother matched my own. They also commented on how dependent she was on the workers.

The father also had a difficult childhood, with his parents splitting up when he was young and both having psychiatric problems, but he had not developed insight in order to acknowledge the impact on his own development. In addition, the parents found it difficult to communicate effectively over important parental tasks, which clearly was of considerable concern.

Care of the children

The report from the organization described a number of areas of concern around the basic care of the children. There was evidence that the couple did not attend to the health needs of the girls, such as not taking them to doctor's appointments when they needed to. Overall, there was the basic difficulty in understanding the children's emotions. There were also some worrying observations about the mother and the children from a play therapist, but no attempt to try to offer an interpretation and shift things along. In addition, there were descriptions of how the two-year-old seemed at times to be invisible to her parents and often in a world of her own. She seemed to have adapted to the insensitive care she had received from her parents by dampening down her natural attachment-seeking behaviour. She also interacted little with either parent, nor did she seek their attention or try to share objects with them. However, the girl was able to respond to positive interaction and enjoyed the active physical game her mother played in one of the sessions. She also enjoyed playing tickling games with her father, when he got the timing right, and she signalled for more. It did seem that the little girl's emotional cues had not been consistently recognized and responded to adequately. There were also comments that the mother would interfere with the flow of the play. The baby was also not given very much active attention, with neither parent having a wide repertoire of ways of stimulating her.

My main point was that the observations were not in dispute, but that there had been no comprehensive attempt to move from observation to intervention. There was clear evidence that the children were suffering emotional harm, and would continue to do so without help. The boy was urgently in great need, not only of a decision about his future placement, but also of intensive therapeutic help for his emotional and behavioural difficulties. But there was no evidence that the girls had been subjected to any physical or sexual abuse, and some evidence that the parents were willing to accept help; indeed, they had fully cooperated with the assessment. I did not feel, given the limited amount of information still available, that I could make a clear judgement about the chances of rehabilitation for this family, but did feel that it was worthwhile proceeding to a fuller assessment to test this out.

Further assessment

Probably because my views conflicted with those of the local authority and the Children's Guardian, who were recommending removal of all the children, the Guardian then instructed another expert to do a full assessment, including the children. At the same time, I was then allowed to see the parents and the girls. In the end, the other expert also recommended removal of the children, and thus a full hearing of the different views took place so that the judge could decide which view would prevail.

My interview with the family took some two and a half hours, during which I observed and recorded in detail the interactions between the parents and the children, talked to the parents on their own and also to the children's social worker.

At the time of the meeting with the parents and the children, "Mary" was aged two and "Sophie" one. Once the children were in my room, Mary went straight for the toys and got the telephone out, while father cuddled both girls and offered a ball to Sophie. Mother played with Mary "Who's on the phone?", and Mary said LaLa and Dipsey were there (*Teletubbies'* characters); and then for about ten minutes Mary played with the tea set. There was no evidence of either parent interfering with the flow of the play, as had been described. Mary made some tea and mother also included Sophie in the game. Mary pretended to drink the tea and stirred it. The girls seemed happy to be with their parents, after some initial hesitation. After about half an hour Mary made increasing eye contact with her mother, while Sophie was at ease from the beginning. Both parents had very clear eye contact with their children and were well focused on them.

Mary gave the cup of tea to her father who said thank you, and then mummy had the cups of tea. There was quite a lot of play between mother and Mary about the tea, cups, etc. Father, meanwhile attended to Sophie, spending quite a lot of time on the floor at her level. She smiled at him as they played a game with the ball. Mary gave father another cup of tea, and mother wondered if she could give me some tea. She first of all said it was for daddy, but then she came up to me with some, which I gratefully accepted. Sophie began to walk a little and also looked at me from time to time. Father then played with Sophie and the phone, and they laughed from time to time.

When Mary gave me yet another cup of tea, I commented on how much she felt she had to feed everyone. It was soon after this comment that mother, who had been sitting on a chair during this time, took Mary on her lap affectionately and then played for some fifteen minutes with the phone. Sophie, meanwhile, had begun to play with a toy train with her father, on the floor.

After a while, Mary began to play with the animals and dolls, and then father, mother and Sophie also played with them, looking at each one in turn. Next, Mary took some paper and started drawing, with the encouragement of both parents. Later, she also played closely with her father; Sophie suddenly became tired (in fact both children had had a long journey to see me), and mother her took in her arms so she could nestle in her lap.

The rest of the contact, which I continued to describe in detail for my report, remained positive. There was no evidence of the children being disturbed, nor any suggestion in that observation of sexualized activity. The play was appropriate and affectionate. The parents were able to help the children return to the foster carer, who had brought the children to the meeting. Of course, it was only a snapshot and took place in a controlled environment. None the less, it was a strange environment for the children, and it is my experience that if there are major problems for the children they usually come out at this point in my assessment. The children were also a little tired after their long journey, and that might have helped to reveal any disturbance. There was also no evidence of any attention deficit or behavioural problems.

After the children had left with the foster carer, I saw the parents on their own. The father was more amenable to looking at their situation realistically. He seemed to understand the seriousness of their situation, and also the fact that they had difficulties as a couple that needed to be looked at. The mother was still rather guarded. But they both admitted that they had been too defensive with regard to professionals. They admitted that they had difficulty opening up because they were afraid that anything they said would be taken and used against them—a common fear. The father felt that they needed help to understand things in layman's terms. He felt that people did not spend enough time and trouble trying to explain things. He wanted more feedback and clearer help about what they could do to change, and more guidance. He particularly wanted help with boundary setting.

I took up with mother how she dealt with her feelings. She agreed that her first reaction was to get defensive and angry rather than look at her own contribution to things. But she also got upset easily, and described how she felt when it was Sophie's first birthday and how upset she was that the child was in foster care.

Overview of family

Overall, my impression of this meeting was that the couple, particularly the father, showed some flexibility, and some willingness to look at their own difficulties. They were not just taking up the entrenched position that they had often taken up before. The main areas of difficulty seemed to be that of boundary setting, which showed itself with the older boy, and also how they tended to get into angry positions with the authorities. The issue of the mother's difficulty in facing her own emotions remained crucial. I noted that she tended to stay on her chair in the contact with the girls, playing but rather aloof. But this changed after I made a comment about Mary having to feed everyone. At that point mother appeared to relax, and was then able to be warmer and less cut off. I think this was evidence that, given the right intervention, mother might be able to shift.

As a result of my further assessment, I was even clearer that the parents and the girls should have the opportunity of being reunited, and that I thought that the chances of this succeeding were reasonably good. The fact that the parents were able to play well with the children, and that they seemed more amenable to accepting they had difficulties that needed to be addressed, were grounds for some optimism.

General considerations

The practice of Social Service departments with regard to families like this varies widely, with differing thresholds for removal of the children. A main issue considered at court was how long one should go on trying to help a family before the children become permanently damaged by the cumulative trauma of parental failure, as was clearly the case with the boy in this family. There was also evidence that the older girl was showing signs of similar damage, while it was too soon to be certain about the baby's damage.

In making decisions about how long one should go on trying to keep children with damaging parents, I have previously indicated (Kennedy, 1997b, p. 85) that a delicate balance has to be drawn up between giving the parents another chance and how this may affect the child's ability to make attachments at any given age. Thus, a baby's needs were the most urgent, because experience has shown that adoptions had a better chance of success when the adoptee is a baby capable of making early, long-lasting attachments. However, with an older child, say, for example, over five years of age, it was probable that there was already long-lasting damage, so that there may not be undue harm if additional time was given to an assessment.

On this basis, one could argue that the boy from this family should be given another chance with the mother and stepfather. However, one also needs to weigh up the degree of disturbance in the child and its cause, the effect in this family of any work with the boy on the potential for helping the other children, and the chances of successfully helping him with his extensive problems. There was agreement by all the professionals that the chances of successfully helping the boy in this family were small, and that trying to do so would produce untold damage in a child who was already deeply troubled. I also felt that there was clear evidence that the boy's difficult behaviour had already interfered with the mother's capacity to look after the girls, as she herself had admitted. But I also felt that there was still some hope of being able to work with her and the girls, once it had been decided not to consider the boy for rehabilitation, however upsetting that might be for the mother. I recommended that whatever was decided about the boy, he urgently needed long-term therapeutic work, preferably including child psychotherapy. I acknowledged that not being reunited with the family was going to be tough for the boy in the short-term, but a relief for him in the long-term, provided he could be found a stable home environment and was also offered appropriate help. I also acknowledged that finally losing her son would be painful for the mother, but necessary if she were to succeed with her girls.

Court hearing

The High Court heard the various arguments for and against my view. Of course, I had to deal with the fact that the other expert and the Guardian wanted the girls to be removed. It is always rather tricky dealing with an expert's report with which one disagrees. One does not want to give the impression that professional rivalry is the basis for a disagreement. In this case, I stuck to the facts as I saw them and the parents' capacities that came out in my interview with them. Because I knew of the other opinions, and because the other expert had not given much actual detail of their interviews, I made sure I recorded as much detail as I could, more so than usual, in order to cite clear clinical evidence for the wisdom of keeping the parents and children together.

In the end, it was not difficult to persuade the judge to send the parents and the girls to a day centre for further work. They received the help they needed there, and the girls were successfully reunited with their parents. The boy was kept in long-term foster care, with some limited contact with the mother, and offered various kinds of help, but I was unable to find out what happened to him.

Second example

Background

This was of an extensive assessment that involved my interviewing the two children, a girl aged twelve and a boy aged ten, caught up in a very worrying situation with their mother and a stepfather, who had allegedly sexually and physically abused the children, and included seeing the children's father and his partner, as well as the children's social worker. I was also sent videos and written transcripts of formal interviews with the children concerning possible physical and sexual abuse.

Instructions

I was asked to carry out a general psychiatric assessment of the mother, to comment on the effects of her relationship with her partner and her ex-husband, and to comment on issues of domestic violence, as well as to carry out a psychiatric assessment of the children, who had been placed in foster care. I was asked to make recommendations about what should happen to the children, and what, if any, interventions should take place to enable the mother to continue to care for them.

Interviews

I began with an extensive interview with the mother, whom I also saw for a follow-up. She came across as very caught up with her relationship with the stepfather, who was in fact in prison on remand for alleged abuse of the children, and unable to believe what her children had revealed about the abuse they had suffered. As far as she was concerned, the allegations were something to with the children's father trying to get at her; she believed that he had coached them.

In fact, as became clear later, it was because the father had re-established contact with the children, after some years, that they were able to talk about their experiences; they at last felt that they had an ally. The father explained to me that the stepfather had been physically threatening to him, and that was one of the reasons that he had stopped trying to see the children. He was also in a new relationship, and had children with his new partner, and so he just gave up. He very much regretted his attitude, and wished he had been more persistent in having contact. I discussed the children's allegations with their mother, such as accusing her partner of hitting them with a belt and putting their heads under water. She said that she thought that none of this was true. She justified this view by telling me that for the last four years the children had been doing well at school. I also went over some of the video evidence with her. She admitted that she had been out of the house most of the day because of her work, and at times when the sexual abuse was alleged to have occurred, but she had absolutely no doubts that it had not occurred.

She did, rather reluctantly, agree that her partner had hit her on a couple of occasions, but that did not mean that he was capable of hitting the children. In general her accounts of her situation and her replies to my questions were presented in a bland way. She did not seem particularly affected by the loss of her children. She showed more irritation with the children than concern that they might be telling the truth, or that there might be some basis for what they were saying.

I went into her background in detail, though it was difficult to elicit much feeling about her family and her development. Both parents were described as hard-working and loyal; but they had had no contact with her since she had been with her partner. Her explanation was that they had offered to look after the children for a while, but then withdrew the offer, and so she cut off contact. She added that until then she had always had a close relationship with her father. This whole episode did seem rather strange. I tried to explore how this sudden cutting off might have had something to do with her partner's behaviour towards them, but I could not clarify this with her.

She had had a series of short-lived relationships with men, including the children's father, until her current partner, whom she described as good with the children, going out with them and playing with them. She also said she had a good relationship with the children, who were loving towards her.

Towards the end of the interview, I tried to press her hard on what was going on. I wondered why she could not admit to herself that something might have been happening.

She said that she was not hiding anything. I pointed out that she was believing her partner and not the children, and I wondered if she could think about that. She added that she had been on bail for aiding and abetting but they had dropped the charges against her as the case was not strong enough. I asked her to think that, if there had been no abuse, why would the children say what they did. She replied that their father was coaching them. She later admitted that she was defending her partner, that she still had feelings for him, and regularly visited him in prison. In fact, as later came out when I saw her some time later for a follow-up, she continued to visit him even though he was also seeing another woman visitor, a new girl-friend.

Overall impression of mother

My overall impression was that her personality was rather shallow emotionally. She tended to be cut off from feelings, particularly with regard to her children. I had a suspicion that she knew what was going on at home, but that she was so besotted with her partner and in need of him that she preferred to take his side rather than have any doubts about him, I should say at this point that eventually my and the other professionals' suspicions were confirmed at court, when it finally came out that the children had indeed been sexually abused, and with the mother's active participation.

Other interviews

I saw the children, their father, his partner, the children's foster carer and the social worker for the children at a local family centre on another day. I made sure that the children were first of all separately accompanied by the social worker, in case there was any pressure from their father to keep to some rehearsed story; and arranged to see the father and his partner after seeing the children. In fact, I found no evidence at all that the children had been coerced or coached by their father.

In my interview with the girl, "Susan", she was able to talk quite openly, after some initial appropriate hesitation. She was an intelligent and thoughtful girl. She had already had formal videotaped interviews about the abuse, so my role was more about trying to get a feel for what she was like rather than to find evidence, but she was quite open about the abuse. She soon told me about the stepfather. To begin with, when her mother first met him some years before, he would tell them off at breakfast for opening a cereal box. But then he got more violent. She got it the most and he sexually abused her. When he hit her and the others he used a shoe, slipper, and belt. He hit them on the backside or the face. This was practically every day, for the smallest thing, such as not putting the dirty washing away. He hit her with a belt and slipper, for example, if they were not quiet while he was trying to sleep. He would tell her to pull down her knickers and use the belt or slipper. The sexual abuse went on from the age of about seven. He would come into her bedroom and tell her to take off her clothes, and then he would get on top of her. He would tell her to suck on his thing. I clarified she meant his penis. He would touch her all over, and put his penis up her thing, that is her vagina, and also her bum. It hurt her, it was painful. The sexual abuse occurred every so often, not every day. I asked if he threatened her, she said no. I asked if she told her mother; she said she hadn't, she never would tell her when he was living there, because it would upset her mother.

However, when he left, she did tell her mother. Her mother cried and was upset, but then he kept phoning, and started coming back on and off, and then mother stopped believing her.

Later in the interview, Susan denied being coached by her father, and, indeed, I had no impression that she had been set up by him.

She seemed genuinely upset by her terrible experiences in the home, and worried about how they were going to affect her future life. She also told me spontaneously that she was keen on seeing a therapist to chat about her worries; for example, about how her experiences might have an effect on her future relationships.

My interview with her ten-year-old brother, "Simon", also revealed a sorry story of physical abuse and the mother's inability to protect the children, although he was more withdrawn than his sister and less able to talk about his feelings. He mainly came alive when I asked him where he would like to live, and he replied, with animation, with his father. In fact, the children had been spending some time at their father's house, with mixed results. There were tensions between them and their step-siblings.

When I talked to their father's partner; she described how Simon had been starved by his mother and sent to his room without food as a punishment. When he visits them he would at first send himself to his room and starve himself if he did some minor thing wrong. To begin with he would also hide under a bed. He would do this even if someone just asked him if he had done his homework. This behaviour had improved, but was still there to some extent.

The partner also described how Susan liked to be in control, and even to try to take over the mothering role with her own children, which had caused tension in the home when the children visited. She told me that Susan had told her that her mother had been in the bedroom when the stepfather was abusing her, and that she was going to admit this formally, in a police interview—which was probably why she had not told me about it; she did in fact do this later. She added that Simon knew all about the abuse, even though he had not admitted this to professionals. She was honest about her own mixed feelings about the issue of having the children live with her, both because of the difficulty in having so many children in one house and the fact that Susan and Simon had suffered such abuse that she was worried about the effect they might have on her own children.

The father struck me as a caring, concerned father, in touch with his children's distress, but also full of guilt about not having inter- vened in the past. He described how difficult it had been for the children. They had been through a lot and they had had nothing. He said that they had never been to a McDonald's before and had never eaten fruit; they didn't even know what a pineapple or a peach was. He described how the picture of extreme neglect at home gradually became clearer the more they saw the children. They never had new clothes, their mother would lie in bed for hours and not get food for them, and would only cook when the stepfather came home, etc.

The problem at his own home was that, when the children visited, Susan was very competitive with one of his other children. Also, since he heard about the sexual abuse he felt himself to be in a difficult position with Susan, for example about giving her a cuddle. The other day he put his arm round her and he felt she was becoming uncomfortable and putting a leg towards him in an inappropriate way. This sounded like evidence of some over-sexualized behaviour. He hadn't actually talked to her directly about this kind of situation, although he managed to push her away as gently as he could.

He expressed a wish for some help about all this. There was no evidence that he was coaching the children to come up with abuse allegations; on the contrary, the allegations had caused considerable trouble in his own home and to him personally.

He felt that he and his partner were coping well, considering, although he added that they had separated briefly because of differences of opinion about how to manage the children. As he continued to talk, I had the increasing impression that the couple were under extreme pressure, and that rather than split up again they might not accept Susan and Simon permanently, not unless some ongoing therapeutic help for the family were arranged as soon as possible. When I saw the couple together, they struck me as decent and caring, honest about their feelings and concerns, but also under considerable strain.

The supportive social worker confirmed this view of the couple, and also that they needed help, but that the local clinic had a few months' waiting list and could not see them soon. So I agreed to write a letter to them, emphasizing the urgency of the situation, and I also talked to the local Consultant over the telephone.

Documents

I was given an extensive series of documents and also a number of videos with their written transcripts. I noted that the mother had described to the social worker how the stepfather had been violent to her and recently, before going to prison on remand, had broken up with her; but she also said repeatedly that she could not accept the children's allegations. She admitted that the stepfather had occasionally gone too far in disciplining them and that she could not stop him. He would take then upstairs to punish them. She was not aware that they had been badly hurt; but nor did she ask them how they were or look to see of there were any marks on them. She admitted that maybe she had not wanted to know. She said that she wanted the children back with her, but, as with me, she expressed no emotion about their experiences or their distress.

The social worker concluded that the mother continued to present as confused and damaged by the experience of domestic violence. It appeared that her own needs prevented her from considering the needs of the children. In addition, father and partner had acted appropriately and in the children's best interests.

The medical examination of the children revealed clear evidence of physical abuse, with scars from injuries, and also evidence of sexual abuse of Susan, with damage to her vagina and anus.

General considerations

One of the questions I was asked in the letter of instructions concerned the effects of domestic violence on the mother and on her capacity to look after the children. Clearly one had to establish whether or not she was as much a victim as her children. Though she might have been a victim in some senses, she was also a participant, and at least negligent in her own right. Once the stepfather was off the scene she did not feel relief, she did not then begin to recapture her reality sense and realize how abused she had been. On the contrary, she continued to be obsessed with him, and to refuse to acknowledge that the children might be telling the truth. I was not convinced that she had merely blanked out the memory of their abuse because she herself had been subjected to violence. Nor was I convinced that her denial was related to a response to a life of violence in the home, though that might have been an element. It seemed more likely that she had turned a blind eye to what was going on because she was besotted with the stepfather, and/or she had participated in the abuse for reasons of her own. There was little doubt that were she to have the children back, they would be put by her into another unsafe position, with the stepfather or another violent man.

Subsequent events

Unfortunately, it was not long before the children's father and his partner made a firm decision not to have Susan and Simon with them on a permanent basis. The family therapy that I had urged had not materialized in time, and the parents felt that the two children created too much disruption to their own home and to their relationship. Thus, by the time of the final hearing, what was at issue was whether or not the mother should have the children returned to her or whether they should remain in long-term fostering with contact with either or both parents. In addition, by that time the mother had been separately charged for the abuse and was awaiting trial.

Court hearing

At the hearing, mother's barrister tried to find fault with my evidence about her and also that of all the other professionals, all of whom considered her to be an unsafe parent, but without success. It became clear that fostering was the only feasible option for the foreseeable future—yet again, the best worst option. There was the issue of the mother's possible contact with the children. As I shall explain in more detail in the following chapter, focused on contact issues, the cardinal rule is that any contact should be in the interests of the children's placement, and would depend upon the relationship between the absent parent and the primary caretakers. At the time of the hearing, both children said that they did not want to see her because of her taking the stepfather's side. I suggested that one should respect their views for the present, but that the situation might change in the coming weeks and months. I also hoped that the children would receive some individual child psychotherapy to address their terrible experiences.

Third example

Instructions

These concerned whether or not a twelve-year-old girl from a strange and very worrying family should be reunited with her mother. Her lawyer instructed me to assess the mother's relationship with the child; her ability to develop and enhance that relationship; her ability to care for the child and meet her needs; what help the mother might need to care for the child and her capacity to cooperate; the prospects of rehabilitation to mother and the likely time scale if this were to happen. If, as the mother was suggesting, she had been the victim of ongoing domestic violence, I was asked to assess the effect this would have on her ability to care for the child and the prognosis for change; and the question of contact if the child were placed outside the family.

Background

The history of recent events in the family had been well summarized by various reports, including that of the social worker and an independent expert instructed by the Guardian. Essentially, social services had been alerted by a member of the community to grave concerns about the family, with the children being physically and emotionally harmed by the father. Once the investigation was started, the mother took an older girl and boy with her, while her youngest, "Sally", was taken into foster care. Another child chose to remain with the father.

From the history I read about and took from the mother and three children, the father seemed to have exerted a sadistic control over the family, terrorizing them and also preventing contact with the outside world, including schools. I was amazed to discover that the children had had hardly any formal education, despite being bright, and that the education authorities had never picked this up. When seen by professionals soon after leaving the home, the mother appeared rather confused and helpless at times, glad to be away from the control of the husband, but appearing vulnerable and uncertain about herself. There were obvious doubts about whether or not she could remain separate from her husband. By the time I saw her she had grown more confident about her abilities as a mother, had begun to live a normal life for the first time in years, and had absolutely no intention of resuming any relationship with her husband. What was clear was that she and the children had been victims of the most severe emotional and physical battering and as a result had been deeply traumatized.

Interview with mother

I saw the mother initially for some two hours, then saw a contact visit between her and her youngest daughter, spoke individually with the two older children who were with the mother, spoke to the social worker, and also did a follow-up meeting with the mother.

Mother came across as intelligent and cultivated, but also somewhat eccentric, with her head rather in the clouds at times. I could see that she might have found it difficult being assertive. However, I also found her focused on her daughter and keen for help. She was having regular contact with her daughter, some of which was unsupervised.

I asked her why Sally was in foster care, and she replied that it was because she herself had not protected her from her father. She then described in detail the kind of life they all lived until she managed to escape from the home. I should say that there was extensive independent evidence of her assertions, and backing from the older children she took with her. She said that he made constant inappropriate sexual comments about the children, even when they were small. For example he would comment on Sally's small breasts, that they would soon be bigger and sexy, and so on. Her own position in the family was eroded over the years so that she was marginalized, as if he were hoping she would simply disappear.

When there were arguments she would get beaten up, for example on the upper arms so that the bruises would not show. He gave that up after a while, but then started various mind games, for example denying food to them and playing one person off against another. There was now a Court Order for him to stop harassing her. She added that he would beat up whoever was in his way, and used the oldest child as his spy; they would listen behind doors. She herself would only have to say a word out of place and he would be violent, smashing up crockery or furniture, for instance.

I asked her why she had put up with all this. She said that she felt it was wrong now, but then she saw no alternative. He would often say that he would have her committed as he was so effective in controlling everything. He controlled what they watched on television; he hated her reading books, so she had to do so in secret. She was not allowed to have the house keys, the house was not in her name, there were never any locks on the doors in the house, so that he could always enter any room he wanted. Now she felt she should have left before, but she had felt that no one would back her up, and she did not want to abandon the children and never see them again. My overall impression was that she was still very traumatized by her experiences in the home, a number of which I am unable to detail in all their horror because of issues of confidentiality. The basic picture was of a family with no privacy or personal space, with the father exerting a relentless dictatorship.

The situation seemed to have worsened since her older boy started becoming independent, when he went to work. This boy became a target of the father's hate, with the father taking all his money and denying him food until at last he ran away, staying with friends. The mother added that none of the children was allowed to go to school—once again I was amazed that this was never picked up by the education authorities.

Mother's background

The mother herself described little physical contact from either parent, though they were caring and good parents. She had a very low opinion of herself and her abilities, even though she went to university and began a good job. Her marriage was her first serious relationship, and she was rather swept off her feet, as he could be quite charming. She had not seen his other side at that time, though she admitted he had thumped her a couple of times before they married.

Overall impression

The mother described how enormously improved her life was since moving out. There was no access to the father and the children did not want to see him, particularly since a meeting with the other expert when the father had come early and whispered in Sally's ear that she should tell them she wanted to live with him. She had good contact with Sally, who was recovering in the foster home. She recognized that Sally had benefited from being there, but she also felt that now was the time for her to return to her family, that is, of course, without the father. The other expert had commented that he was struck by the mother's passivity and lack of anger in respect of her marriage and the experiences of her children within the family. But by the time I saw her, this had changed somewhat in that she certainly displayed to me anger about what had happened to them all, and a regret about her lack of assertiveness. But she still came across as rather passive, with difficulty in exerting her own authority as a mother. Her somewhat distant relationship to her own mother might have contributed to this attitude. As a result of not being with her abusive husband, she was quite willing to accept help for herself and her children. She had certainly been traumatized by her experiences, but was beginning to recover. I certainly felt that she needed counselling or therapy, both individually and within the family setting, in order to deal more effectively with the trauma and also to help her with the children.

Contact visit

I next saw a contact visit between mother and Sally. I was explicitly told not to do a detailed interview with the girl as this had already been done by the other expert. In fact, I found her easy to talk to and not particularly worried by my presence in the room observing the two of them. As I had also arranged to talk to the two children living with the mother, they had all come together, and when I arrived at the contact centre all the children were happily talking to one another in a relaxed and chatty way. But what I noticed with the children was a somewhat artificial and stilted way of talking, presumably related to the fact that they had never engaged in normal social life with others.

During the contact observation Mother and Sally spent the time well together, doing some school work and also some playing. At one point when the mother became somewhat fussy and over-anxious, Sally told her rather tetchily that she shouldn't fuss. But then they settled down again to some painting, with the mother helping out with the mixing of colours. When I spoke to the social worker later in the day, she mentioned that early contacts had been quite difficult, as Sally had been very testing of her mother and the mother found it difficult standing up to her. However, mother was now more able to take charge of situations, as I witnessed myself.

Interviews with the other children

The interviews with the other children confirmed more of their traumatic upbringing, as well as the relative normality of their current life with their mother, and their wish to obtain some formal education for the first time in their lives. One of the children claimed that the father heard voices and talked to angels and devils, giving the impression that the father was a paranoid schizophrenic. The girl implied that there might have been sexual abuse, though she was unwilling to talk about this issue in detail. What she did say was that the father would show them, including Sally, sick pornographic films. She explained that he wanted Sally to watch them in order to prime her up for later. Neither older child was keen on individual therapy, perhaps because they were afraid it might stir up too much emotional pain, but they all agreed to participating in family work, if it would help their mother get Sally back.

Documents

The other expert's report described detailed family functioning nearer the time when the mother had left the home. He noted that the mother and older brother and sister tended to play down the need to talk about their past, and to make it seem more positive than it was, which was confusing Sally. He noted Sally's expressed wish to return to the care of her mother, but it was not clear to what extent she was being influenced by the rest of the family's attempts to re-edit the past. He also saw the oldest child, who had remained with the father, and who was strongly identified with him, denying that there was anything wrong in the family. He also observed how mother had developed a way of cutting off emotionally, although I myself noted that this had shifted somewhat, now that she had been away from the father for some months. The father had also been seen, and he came across as having considerable personality difficulties.

I certainly agreed that it was right for Sally to be placed in the foster home, where she would be exposed to normal family life and other children. At the time she went to the foster home there was great concern about mother's ability to effectively separate from the father and to prioritize her daughter's needs. There was now an issue about whether or not there was an opportunity for the mother to have Sally back, but if so how this should be done and at what pace.

Answers to instructions

With regard to my instructions, I thought that the relationship between mother and Sally was a good and close one; they were able to talk to one another well, and mother related to her appropriately. In the contact visit they were generally relaxed and the mother could play well with her. The situation had improved from before, when Sally was challenging and mother could not stand up to her effectively. Clearly, mother had some limitations based on her own distant early mothering experiences. The main issue, of course, was that the mother had allowed the family to be dominated by the father in highly abnormal ways. There were major concerns about her ability to develop and enhance the children's relationships because of this. However, my own impression was that, given a certain amount of help, mother could develop her abilities—she had already shown improvement in this area in the previous months. I suggested that the family would need a package of support and therapeutic work, including some individual and family work, if the return of Sally to her mother's care was to succeed. I also recommended that the rehabilitation work should begin as soon as possible.

There was also the issue of mother having been the victim of ongoing domestic violence, which had had a major impact on her ability to care for Sally. She was unable to provide a safe environment while under the domination of her husband. However, away from the situation, she had greatly improved, and she had showed over several months no wish to return to him, unlike the mother in my second example. She was beginning to make a life for herself and to enjoy her new-found freedom. Such an attitude would suggest that the prognosis for lasting change was reasonably good. I also added that if Sally were to be placed outside the family, she would need to have ongoing contact with her mother and siblings, as they clearly had a strong relationship with one another.

Court hearing

When I gave evidence at the final hearing, father's barrister gave me a very difficult time. He was quite aggressive, in a somewhat inappropriate way, perhaps mirroring his client's personality. Of course, he wanted to challenge my clinical views, asserting that the story from the mother and the children was a pack of lies, aimed simply at hurting his client. The older sibling had already testified to that effect. I just stuck to the evidence as I saw it, which was pretty clear and damming. I emphasized the issue of domestic violence and bullying, and the clear evidence of damage to the children, and pointed to the result of their lack of formal education. I was cross-examined at length about the issue of the mother's ability to look after children, about which there was still, after all, some doubt. However, I was aided by the fact that the other expert and I were in agreement that rehabilitation should be attempted, so long as it were done with good therapeutic resources and over a period of three months or so.

After a long hearing, lasting well over a week, the judge decided to go for the rehabilitation option, and denied the father any direct contact with Sally. I later heard that Sally was successfully returned to her mother and the family were doing well in their community, though the father continued, unsuccessfully, to try to overturn the court's decision.

CHAPTER FOUR

Contact issues

General points

C
ontact between children and the parent who is not their
primary carer is desirable in principle but often fraught
with complex issues that may have to be addressed before
such contact can take place. The decisions that have to be made
about such contact include its frequency and whether or not it is
direct, that is face to face, or indirect, through letter or telephone
contact; whether or not it is supervised or unsupervised, and where
it should take place. Such decisions can usually be taken by social
services in consultation with the parents. However, there are occasionally times when an expert is called in to give advice, particularly when there is some dispute between the various parties about
aspects of the contact, whether or not it should be direct or indirect,
supervised or unsupervised, or whether or not is should take place
at all.

In principle, any decisions about contact should be flexible, as
situations involving contact disputes change over time. A parent
who is initially intransigent about contact arrangements, particularly soon after a decision affecting their care of their child has been

taken, may be full of anger and bitterness about the decision, making it difficult for them to see what is in the child's best interest rather than their own. However, their attitude may change once the dust has settled. A parent who is mentally ill and unable to care for their child may be able to keep up contact when they are well, but not when they are ill again. Another parent who may be unstable and unreliable over keeping up regular contact may eventually settle down. From the child's point of view, they may wish to change any contact arrangements as they grow up and can decide for themselves whether or not they wish to see an absent parent and for how long. Setting up contact arrangements in stone is to be done only as a last resort, when all possibility of negotiation has broken down. In addition, there is the basic principle that must also be taken into account: that any contact should *not jeopardize* the child's new placement, should not cause the placement undue disruption. Making a decision about whether or not there should be contact and what kind and at what level must also take into account the effect on the child's new home. How much weight one attaches to this factor will depend on the age of the child and the reasons for their removal from the parent's care. While the absent parent should in principle be able to see their child reasonably frequently, this may not be in the child's best interests, at least in the early stages of a new placement.

The principles underlying decision making about contact issues are well summarized in a paper by Claire Sturge and Danya Glaser (2000), after they were asked by the Court of Appeal for guidance on a difficult domestic violence case. They describe the core principles that should guide decisions as being determined in all cases by the best interests of the child. Decisions about contact should be child-centred and relate to the specific child and their specific situation at the time.

The different *purposes* of contact include the sharing of information and knowledge, which can help the child's sense of identity; to maintain meaningful and helpful relationships; to give an experience of being loved and being the focus of attention, which can be beneficial for the child's emotional growth and development; to repair broken or problematic relationships; to give the child an opportunity of reality testing; to facilitate the assessment of the quality of the relationship or contact when a return to a parent is being assessed, or a change in contact arrangements is being proposed; and in severing relationships, for example at a goodbye meeting.

The benefits of direct contact include:

- the warmth and approval unique and special to a parent;
- extending experiences and developing or maintaining meaningful relationships;
- information and knowledge;
- reparation of distorted relationships.

The usefulness of indirect contact includes:

- experience of the interest of the absent parent, so as to minimize the child feeling responsible for the breakdown of their relationship;
- knowledge and information about the absent parent;
- keeping open the possibility of the relationship developing at some future date—an opportunity, through letters or phone calls, for reparation.

Assessing the risks involved in direct and indirect contact includes looking at the weight to be attached to factors such as domestic violence, and the absence of any meaningful bond to the absent parent, as well as disruption to the new placement.

Contact disputes can arise at any stage after the breakdown of family relationships, whether from separation and divorce or when a child is removed from the family home. Particularly common times for these to occur include the period of the initial breakdown, the introduction of new partners, changes of residence by either partner, negotiations over financial issues, and an adolescent child testing out boundaries. Ideally, these disputes should be resolved by negotiation and agreement. It is certainly in the child's best interests to know that their parent or parents can take adult responsibility by forging mutually acceptable agreements about their child. This can be particularly difficult when social services are also involved, and when the professionals have already had to deal with the family and remove children from their parents' care. Lawyers may then be brought in to mediate between parties, but the law can also be used to perpetuate disputes.

I would suggest that there is a problem in using the law to resolve these kinds of dispute, in that because English law is essentially adversarial there is a natural tendency for it to perpetuate ongoing fights rather than promote the resolution of conflicts. While the court can provide a containing function for the various parties, that is, a place where conflicts can be heard and ideally resolved, it can also provide a battleground for the playing out of the bitter disputes that led to the breakdown of the couple's relationship. This is most relevant in private law disputes, where couples would be better advised to sort things out for themselves. It would certainly save a lot of money. However, contact disputes following the removal of children are generally of such a complex nature that it may well be necessary to use the court process to weigh up the needs of the children.

The dynamics of contact disputes are usually quite complex, especially when they interact with the dynamics of the court process. The wish to perpetuate old fights rather than lay down arms in order to help the children is unfortunately common in those disputes that reach the court. While the court ultimately has a certain amount of power—though often less in reality than in fantasy—the use of this power, for example to enforce contact orders, may not necessarily facilitate any change in the situation. As Lord Justice Thorpe has indicated in Re L, V, M and H (Contact: domestic violence) [2000] 2 FLR 334 and 366, the court's powers were restricted to regulating the mechanism of contact and did not extend to the underlying relationships between the parties and the child. He questions in this judgement whether the investment of public funds in litigation in order to resolve contact disputes was productive, rather than use treatment resources. The recent setting up of the Children and Family Court Advisory and Support Service (CAFCASS) is now meant to help resolve these kinds of problem more effectively, before using up court time.

My own approach to assessing contact disputes is to see if it is at all possible to resolve them by the parties talking to one another. However, it is often the case that by the time they have come to an expert the bitterness between the parents is such that no amount of conciliation is possible. The factors that led to the breakdown of the parental relationship may still dominate the way that the parties deal with their children. Nevertheless, I still attempt to start a resolution process. Whether or not this is possible then becomes part of the assessment. Such a process, which one hopes may lead to some form of shared, child-focused tasks, may take some time and effort to get going. It may be particularly difficult to get the parties together when, as is more and more often the case, there are multiple relationships and interests involved; for example, with many siblings from different relationships, reconstituted families, and thus complex loyalty issues. Allowing the child to have their own view, if they are old enough to have one, is crucial in the assessment process, but difficult when all around are in dispute for their own reasons.

The court can be turned to in order to seek revenge for, or "judgement" about, the breakdown of the relationship, rather than to help the children. Thus, any effective assessment of contact disputes needs to attempt to disentangle past disagreements that led to the breakdown of the relationship from current contact disputes; that is, to attempt to help the parties let go of the past, come to terms with the loss of the relationship, however awful it may have been, and to accept the new reality of needing to help the children's confusion, upset, and conflicting loyalties. It certainly does not help the children resolve their difficult feelings about the breakdown of their parent's relationship when they see them still at war. A main aim of the assessment, then, is to help the parties listen to the voice of the child.

There are two particular areas which frequently come before the courts for resolution—contact disputes involving domestic violence, and the intransigent parent.

Domestic violence

I take such violence to refer to physical, sexual, or emotional abuse within a domestic or family setting. Emotional abuse in this context would involve intimidation, harassment, threats, damage to property, and may involve direct or indirect abuse of children. Accurate rates of such violence are difficult to ascertain because of under-reporting, but research suggests that about a quarter of all women may experience some domestic violence during their lifetime. Domestic violence is usually perpetrated by men on women, though it can also be perpetrated by women on men and on one another. It accounts for a quarter of all violent crime, and two out of five murders of women in England and Wales are by partners or ex-partners. Women also have twice the risk of experiencing domestic violence when they are pregnant. Some 750,000 children witness domestic violence, and 75% of children on the "at risk" register live in homes where such violence occurs. Children are most vulnerable to abuse and long-term adverse effects when domestic violence co-exists with parental mental illness or alcohol and/or drug abuse.

Understanding such violence is a complicated matter, and with the multi-problem family cannot always be simply divided into a male abuser and a female victim; instead, one is often required to try to make sense of a violent relationship involving both partners.

Even when the male is the main perpetrator, the woman may be involved in violence towards her children, as in the second example of the previous chapter. This pattern is different from those situations that tend to come more to the notice of the police, where a violent male intimidates and beats up a vulnerable female partner, who needs to escape with her children. We do now hear more often about women who have been directly violent to men, though this is a controversial area; there is a danger that pointing this out may help to minimize the severe risk that many women run of being badly injured by their violent partners. None the less, it would seem to be wise to keep the definition of domestic violence fairly wide. Certainly the kind of domestic violence seen in mental health settings may be different from what comes to the immediate attention of the police, with more complex couple issues than one partner being violent to their innocent victim.

Of course, it is difficult to separate violence within the family from social factors influencing the family. In a society where violent acts are celebrated regularly in the media, where gangster movies or television series are both popular and highly entertaining, where smacking of children is seen as normal across all classes, where social deprivation is widespread with all its attendant disadvantages, including criminality and institutionalized violence, it is hardly surprising that violence within the family is a regular problem.

However, it is difficult to tease out what factors have most influence on creating such violence. It is probably the case that there is a complicated interaction between individual, family, and social factors. However much one has to attend to the individual and family factors in assessing situations of domestic violence, it is difficult to completely eliminate all the wider social issues from the picture.

In the multi-problem family one can see a number of patterns that seem to be associated with various kinds of violence, both between a couple and from one or more parent towards their children. Such patterns include insecure and distorted attachments, difficulties in tolerating dependency and vulnerability, breakdown of everyday family functions, intergenerational conflict, merging and blurring of child–parent boundaries, problems in using symbolic structures to contain anxieties so that acting out rather than thinking dominates functioning, use of primitive defence mechanisms to deal with anxieties within the family such as splitting, scapegoating, and massive projection, and the presence of unmetabolized traumas, including a history of childhood abuse in one or both parents. Such patterns predispose to violent acts, particularly at times of stress, so that the families no longer become protective havens and springboards for development. Treatment of such families can be difficult and demanding, involving staff having to process powerful feelings and anxieties in themselves, for which adequate training and supervision is ideally necessary.

In making clinical judgements about contact in these kinds of family, there are the general issues about what is in the child's best interest to take into account, already summarized above; and then there are specific issues arising from a violent home. The latter are well summarized in a report, *Contact Between Children and Violent Partners* (1999), given to the Lord Chancellor by the Children Act Subcommittee of the Advisory Board on Family Law, chaired by Mr Justice Wall. They recommend that in each case where a finding of domestic violence has been made by the court, the court should consider a number of *specific* issues. These include considering the conduct of both parents towards one another and towards the children, and in particular the effect of the domestic violence on the child and on the parent with whom the child is living; whether or not the motivation of the parent seeking contact is a desire to promote the best interests of the child, or as a means of continuing the violence and intimidation of the other parent and children; the likely behaviour of the parent seeking contact during contact and its effect on the child; the capacity of the parent seeking contact to appreciate the effect of past and future violence on the other parent and the child; the attitude of the parent seeking contact to past violence by that parent, and their capacity to change and/or behave appropriately. The report emphasizes that a crucial part of any assessment for contact is to see how much *responsibility* an offender takes for their violent behaviour as an indicator of an ability to change their behaviour in the future.

Once the court had decided in favour of direct contact, then it should also consider whether or not contact should be supervised; what conditions, such as seeking advice or treatment, should be complied with by the parent seeking contact; whether or not the court should make a specific non-molestation order, with penalties for failure to comply; whether such contact should be for a specified period or should contain provisions having effect for a specific period; and whether to set a date for reviewing the whole situation.

The intransigent parent

Intransigent parents are those parents who refuse to cooperate with contact arrangements, either voluntarily agreed or imposed by the court. This can refer, for example, to a father who will not abide by clear guidelines for contact, or to a mother who refuses to allow the father regular contact despite court orders. Such situations can be difficult to resolve, particularly if the primary caretaker is determined not to allow the child to see the absent parent. Even when a court orders contact to take place, the determined parent can find ways to prevent regular contact, and, not surprisingly, courts are reluctant to use threats of imprisonment, particularly against mothers, to make the parent conform to a contact order. When assessing these situations, one is looking to see how unreasonable is the parent who refuses contact, or more often, makes contact difficult or less frequent than it should be. Ideally, mediation should be used to attempt to resolve these situations, but the courts may still have to take an active role in trying to re-establish appropriate contact. The problem for, say, the father in these circumstances, is how much to push the mother into agreeing to the established arrangements when the child may then suffer as a consequence; the temptation for some fathers is just to give up trying to see their children.

It sometimes happens that the children themselves absolutely refuse to see the absent parent, even when contact has been agreed by both parties. The assessment in these circumstances will include trying to judge how much this view genuinely comes from the child and how much they are responding to the caretaker parent's views of the absent parent.

Examples

Example one: clear domestic violence

BACKGROUND AND INSTRUCTIONS

The first example illustrates a violent father and a victimized mother and her two children, a girl aged five and a boy aged three, where the father was asking for direct contact with his children. However, as a result of the continued risk of further direct violence to the mother, my assessment recommended that there should be no direct contact. I was helped in preparing my report by the fact that a judge had already made findings of fact in regard to the father's violence, although the father continued to deny it. My instructions included thirteen questions concerning the issue of contact, the effect of the violence on the children, and the effect any possible contact might have on their future development.

Before seeing the family, I read through the various documents, which gave a clear picture of a long history of the father's intimidation of, and attacks on, the mother, sometimes in front of the children. Indeed, by the time I was instructed, mother and the children were living in a refuge in another city at an address unknown to the father. The judge commented that he had not the slightest doubt that this was a case where the husband had frequently meted out violence to his wife. The father also had a long criminal history, including crimes of violence.

Clearly, with this history, there was no question of seeing mother and father together, at least in the first place and until the father's current state of mind had been assessed. Nor was there any question of organizing a meeting to view contact between him and the children until he had been seen, in order to assess the wisdom of putting the children through what might be a disturbing and even dangerous process. Thus, I initially offered to see the mother and the children and then the father on separate days. However, as it turned out I never got to see the father. I offered several appointments, and I also offered to travel to see him at a neutral (and safe) location. I received his first excuse for not coming the day before the appointment—the message was that he was due in court. I sent him two other appointments, but he never confirmed that he would come, and in the end I made my report without seeing him. His behaviour towards the assessment made it even more obvious what should happen, but there were still questions to be answered about the state of the children, their own wishes, and what help they and the mother might need in the future.

INTERVIEW WITH MOTHER AND CHILDREN

Mother and the children were accompanied by their solicitor. I saw the mother on her own first, and then saw the children with her for a family interview. I had kept in mind the possibility of seeing the children on their own, but in the end I judged that this was unnecessary, as the picture was clear enough from seeing them altogether.

PRESENTING PROBLEMS

I asked the mother why she had come to see me. She said that the children had seen everything that the father had done to her. Any problems they have and the difficulties in the family situation were down to his violence. The boy had temper tantrums and had been copying his father's behaviour. For example, he once pinned his sister against a wall, had used knives, and put a screwdriver to his sister's face. He calmed down once his father went to prison. When they first went into the refuge, he chased other children around the garden with a carving knife, repeating things his father said, such as when his father called her a whore. He was too young to understand what the words meant, but it was still worrying. However, now he was much calmer, and more open with people. Before, he would not let them play with him, but he was now more trusting.

She told me that her daughter used to wet the bed five to six times at night, when they were at home. She used to have stomach aches and was distant and withdrawn. She now had speech therapy and educational help. Mother claimed that the girl's development was affected when the father came out of prison when she was about eighteen months old. Her development seemed to stop; she stopped talking, clammed up, and hardly spoke. But, like her brother, she was now much more open and trusting of people.

DETAILS OF VIOLENCE

We then went into the details of the violence in the home. She said that when she first knew her husband she knew about his criminal background but not about the violence. He seemed such a nice person, despite everything. One day, soon after they were together, there was a violent incident. He accused her of going out with another man, grabbed her by the hair, ripped the buttons off her coat and punched her on the arms. The violence was then continuous, only interrupted by his various periods in prison. There was verbal abuse and also punching and slapping. When he was in prison he would threaten her that one of his mates would come and do her if she did not behave. The slaps soon turned to kicks and punches—on the head, back, tops of legs, all the areas that were covered and would not show. He was violent in front of the children on many occasions. I asked what she did to try to protect them. She said that she tried putting them upstairs, then they would scream and try to stop him from hitting her, or they would stay on the settee and cry, desperately worried about her.

I asked if he had ever hit the children. She replied that he had been rough with her son and had once pinned him down with his hands over his mouth, and had slapped him hard on a couple of occasions resulting in bruising. Once, they were in the kitchen with her son and then she wanted to put him to sleep. The father then felt she was paying more attention to the boy than to him, so he resented this and picked him up and chucked him on the settee, whacking him and calling him a fucking little bastard, and saying he'd put him in care. She then answered him back, and because she stuck up for her son he told her she was going to get it, and he beat her up. Another time, one night, the boy was whining a bit and he said, "Can't we shut this kid up?" She said he was just a baby. Then the father grabbed a cup of tea and chucked it over her, grabbed the child and put his hand over his mouth, trying to stifle his cries. He threatened her that he was going to get the children taken off her as she could not look after them. His attitude was that he could do what he wanted with his children and it was good to toughen them up. He once thwacked the boy very hard and drew blood on his bottom and back. I asked if he ever hit his daughter. She said that he once smacked her violently. There was a stereo on a shelf, and she was messing about and pulled a wire. Mother said no to her, and he then whacked the girl on the top of her legs. He often said to the girl that she was stupid like her mother.

The father was no help in the home, he wouldn't ever clear up his plates, she had to wait on him hand and foot, he even expected her to flush the toilet for him. Sometimes she tried to have a conversation with him to sort things out, but he would never apologize and never wanted to talk about their problems. There was also no affection in their sexual relationship, though no actual violence.

I wondered when she had decided to leave. She said that she had always wanted to leave but feared the consequences as he had threatened to kill one of the children or her family, whom he had already intimidated. The night before she left he had given her something to wash, but in the morning he could not find it as it was still in the washing machine. He went mental and screamed abuse, while the children ran about screaming. She ran out of the front door and said he could not keep intimidating her. He insisted she come back in the house, but as she did he picked up a knife and charged towards her. She slammed the door shut, while the children were banging on the window and crying for her. She went to get help from her family. I wondered why she had not contacted the police, She replied that she thought it might make matters worse because she wanted to get the children out. When she returned a couple of hours later with support he had taken the children to his parents. He refused to give them back and said she would never see them again. In fact, he was forced by the court to return to them to her care two days later. Then she went into a refuge, and the children had not seen him since.

MOTHER'S BACKGROUND

I next went into her own background. Her father had left her mother when she was a baby. He had tried to kidnap her, but without success, and since then there had been no contact. He would beat up her mother. She herself was close to her stepfather, whom she saw as her real father. She and the mother tended to clash from time to time, but otherwise they were a close family.

I eventually wondered why she had become involved with problem men—her husband was not the first, though the first to hit her—and she thought it was probably because she fell for their charm. I wondered if she saw a link with the fact that her natural father had beaten up her mother. She did not really know about this as he left years ago. Clearly, if there were a link, which I thought was most likely, it was deeply unconscious. I asked her if she would like counselling or therapy to try and sort out some of her difficulties, including her attachments to problem men, and she agreed she would and had, indeed, already received some counselling from the refuge.

FAMILY INTERVIEW

I went into the details of the children's development, and then I saw them with her. She was encouraging of them and also firm when necessary. There was clearly a good relationship between her and them and there seemed no obvious sign of any acute disturbance. However, the girl still showed some speech delay, and the boy began to become increasingly restless as the interview progressed. The mother explained that he could not stand being enclosed for a long time, and towards the end of the interview she had to work hard to keep him from trying to rush out of the room. He also had difficulties in keeping focused on one task at a time.

THE DOCUMENTS

The documents showed that there was clear evidence to back up the mother's descriptions of a long history of domestic violence, denied repeatedly by the father. The judge hearing the situation made a clear judgement in favour of the mother's view. There was clear evidence of physical violence against mother and also verbal abuse, which took place on occasion in front of the children, and also when the children were about the house and aware of what was happening.

Conclusions

I then came to my conclusions. I began by going through the general issues about contact on the lines indicated above as guidance about making recommendations in this particular situation.

I then recommended that, given the fact that the court had found for the mother with regard to the domestic violence and did not believe the father's constant denials about it, it would be a very risky undertaking indeed for the father to have direct contact with the children at that time. The children had witnessed repeated domestic violence over a number of years. Clearly they had been considerably disturbed by the home environment. It was only the fact that they had been in a safe refuge for six months that had helped them come to terms with what had happened to them, thus allowing them to become more manageable away from the violence. It seemed clear from a clinical point of view that one could not be satisfied that the safety of the mother and children could be maintained if direct contact were allowed.

In addition, if direct contact were allowed, one could not rule out the children becoming disturbed again, owing to the memories of being hit and witnessing violence being reawakened. However, the main point was to see whether the motivation of the father in seeking contact was a desire to promote the best interests of the children, or a means of continuing a process of violence, intimidation, or harassment of the mother. Given the fact that the father denied his violence, and the fact that the mother indicated quite clearly the level of the threats to which she had been subjected, one could not help but wonder whether the father really wished contact in order to continue this process of violence. While I myself was unable to see the father in order to test out directly how much he could change and acknowledge his own difficulties and the effect of his behaviour on his wife and children, it seemed most unlikely from all the other evidence that he could so change. He had certainly showed no evidence of a wish to change because he revealed no willingness to acknowledge the seriousness of his behaviour.

ANSWERS TO INSTRUCTIONS

I was asked a number of questions, which indicate the kind of issues that often need to be addressed at court in these difficult situations.

The first question concerned the nature and extent of any behavioural problems exhibited by the children. It was, of course, difficult to be too precise about such problems as the result of a one-off interview, particularly as the children had a long way to travel to see me and might have been rather tired. The girl's speech was immature and she had long way to go in order to catch up with her educational attainments. The boy seemed the most vulnerable in that he had difficulty in focusing for a length of time, and had to be encouraged a lot by the mother to sit down and play. Given encouragement he was able to do so quite well, but according to his mother his behaviour had been a lot worse in the past—confirmed by various reports—and he was only now settling down because of the stability offered by the refuge.

In the second question I was asked about the possible causes of any behavioural problems, particularly in relation to the history of the marriage and the violence witnessed by the children. Quite clearly, any difficulties that the children had experienced were very much related to this kind of violence, and the tense emotional atmosphere surrounding the home environment. The girl's developmental delay may have been related to the emotional harm she had suffered, and, in addition, the mother described how the father constantly undermined the girl's confidence. The mother also described how the boy had begun to imitate his father's threatening attitude. It is certainly true that one commonly sees behavioural difficulties in children in violent households. In this case, the children witnessed actual physical harm and were occasionally subjected to it, but also they were subjected to a harmful atmosphere of harassment, intimidation, and threats.

The third question was whether or not I needed to observe face to face contact between the children and the father. Initially, I had kept an open mind about this issue, wanting to see the father for myself in order to ascertain if he were amenable to shifting in his attitude now that the judge had found that he had been violent to his family. I certainly had no intention of observing such contact without seeing him first and without assessing the mother and the children. It was my view that I did not need to see such contact to know that the father had intimidated his family. I considered that the information that would be given to me as a result of seeing this contact would not be of sufficient importance to put the children through what might have been a traumatic contact session—traumatic in the sense that they might worry that they would be returning to the family home, or that the father would be having them back.

The fourth question asked about the children's capacity to relate to the adult world and their ability to benefit from contact with the father in that context. The children showed a capacity to relate reasonably well. However, while it might be beneficial in principle for children to have contact with their father, one had to weigh this up against the danger to them, both physically and emotionally.

I was asked in the fifth question to take account of the children's ages, and then whether their need for consistency, security, and stability would be disturbed by having direct contact with their father, whether they were capable of building a relationship with him, and whether he was capable of building a relationship with them. Quite clearly I believed that the need of the children for consistency, security, and stability would definitely be disturbed by direct contact with their father at this time. I was not sure whether or not they and he would be able to build a better relationship. This would require a considerable shift on his part. He would have to acknowledge what he had done and be willing to talk to professionals about how to talk to the children, as well as how to deal with his anger. I recommended that this would be the minimum expectation before he had any chance of re-establishing direct contact with them.

The sixth question concerned whether the children were likely to have been affected by the attitude and concerns of their mother in connection with contact with their father. Quite clearly this was likely to be the case, and rightly so, given the fact that the judge had ruled that the mother had been subjected to repeated violence. In addition, I saw no evidence in my meeting with the family that the mother was actively poisoning the children against the father. On the contrary, she was if anything trying to avoid talking much about him because of the pain that it might cause.

In the seventh question I was asked about what steps could be taken by the parents to minimize any distress or behavioural reactions on the children's part that might be connected with contact and the attitude of the adults to such contact. Both parents would need to put the children's point of view and their needs first.

However, since I recommended there should be no contact, this question was not relevant.

The eighth question dealt with the issue of potential risks to the children in having contact with their father, and whether these outweighed the benefits. Clearly, I thought that there were real risks of continued intimidation and harassment. I also thought that there were risks to the children's emotional well-being. I felt that they needed stability and a long period of time without being subjected to any possibility of harassment.

I was asked in the ninth question what were the risks of the children having contact, and the risks of having contact refused. If contact were refused there was the risk that the children would begin to forget their father and that his influence would gradually wane. While children need to have a relationship with their father if at all possible, this should not be at any price. The father in this case would have to deal with the fact that he had been violent and that there are consequences to his actions. If that meant that he would become less important to his children then that would be something he had to live with. However, I also thought that the children were going to need help to understand what had happened, as they would inevitably tend to blame themselves for what had happened.

If face to face contact were not at this stage in the children's best interests, the tenth question asked how soon this should be reviewed, and whether there should be indirect contact in the intervening period. I thought that it would be helpful for the children to have some indirect contact through letters, presents, etc. At least then the children would realize that their father was alive and was concerned about them. However, I also suggested that this material be carefully monitored before being given to the children. It should also be explained to the children that they would not be seeing their father for the foreseeable future and why. I suggested that it would be safe to review the situation annually.

The eleventh question asked whether or not this father had the ability to change his behaviour and his attitude to violence. Clearly, my answer was negative.

The twelfth and final question asked whether direct contact would affect the children if the mother had a genuine fear of the father. Clearly, direct contact would affect the children if she had such a genuine fear, because she had real reasons for fear in view of the violence she had been subjected to. I could also imagine that her realistic anxiety would indeed transmit itself to the children, and that this would be quite natural.

In the end, the father was refused direct contact, and monitored, indirect contact was allowed.

Example two: reluctant children

The background concerns an unfortunate situation where two children, a boy aged eleven and a girl aged nine, refused to have contact with their mother. The children were living with their father a couple of years after the break-up of the marriage. Initially, the children remained with their mother, while having frequent direct contact with the father. But when the father remarried, the children eventually decided to live with him and his new wife, and soon refused to see their mother, supposedly because she had been bullying and threatening to them. Various attempts were then made to repair the relationship between the mother and children, including the intervention of CAFCASS, but without success. The parents remained barely on speaking terms and the children were adamant that they would not see their mother, even at a contact centre. The mother alleged the father had turned the children against her, while the father blamed her aggressive behaviour for their attitude towards her. I was then brought in to address the issue of contact between the children and their mother and any other matters relating to the children's welfare.

The parents agreed with my proposal to see the mother first, followed by the father, and then, after an interval, both parents together to see if there could be any shift in the current situation as well as to assess ongoing problems. I thought it important to see both parents before interviewing the children in view of the intractable nature of the problems.

Interview with mother

PRESENTING PROBLEMS

Mother, in her late thirties, told me that the children had left home a year before to live with their father. She had no idea why. She said that there had been some sort of argument with the boy, then his father had phoned up to say that he was upset and was staying overnight, to which she agreed. After a couple of days he had not returned, and this carried on for two weeks or so. Her daughter was clinging on to her during that time, wanting her brother back. Then one evening she had some homework to do, became upset and went to her father's. The daughter told the father that her mother had shouted at her, which was untrue, and she stayed with him. She had not seen the children since then.

She had been to solicitors, the courts and CAFCASS, but nothing had been resolved. I asked her why not. She said again that she did not know. The children want to live with their father. She had agreed, provided she has contact. I asked her what their father had said about the children's attitude. He said that they had no interest in seeing her. They have said that she kicked them in the face once and that she had even tried to strangle her son; again, all this was untrue. Mother described the attempt at CAFCASS to have contact with her. There were two attempts, when the children refused to come. At the third attempt, they were badly behaved, threw toys at the walls and refused to have a conversation. I asked her about her ex-husband's new family. He had remarried A, who had children of her own; she had not spoken to A, who used to be a friend. She added that apparently the children do get on with her and her own children. She then described what sounded like a complete breakdown of communication between her and her ex- husband. She was never given information about the children's welfare.

MOTHER'S BACKGROUND

I then asked her about her own background. Her parents were unhappy, often shouting and fighting. She had not talked to her mother since her marriage since she was always interfering; she was described as not warm or particularly loving, although there was no physical abuse. The father, who died some years before, was described as quiet, loving, and always there for her. She was close to a brother whom she often saw. She had no school problems and went to work soon after leaving school.

HER MARRIAGE

The marriage was fine to begin with. He was kind, generous, and thoughtful. She described her pregnancies, which were difficult, but she was happy to have the children, and there was no depression following their births. She added later that when the children lived with her, after he had left, she always made sure he was given copies of the school reports, but she had not received any since the children had been living with him. I was rather surprised by this, and asked if she herself had asked for them directly from the school. She said she had not. I asked her why not, and she could not explain this. I thought this was quite significant. There was a passive quality in the mother's attitude. Instead of complaining about not receiving reports from her ex-husband, she could simply have telephoned the school.

We returned to the marriage, and she explained that in the last couple of years of their relationship the cracks opened up and they drifted apart. He was always out, leaving her with the children, until he eventually moved out. While he said that he was not in a relationship, she had great doubts about this. The children had daily contact with him, first at the marital home and then at his new place. She was not upset about the break-up of the marriage, though she was annoyed that he had married a friend of hers.

MOTHER AND CHILDREN

I then went into how things had been with the children. I asked how she managed when they were naughty. She said that she had lost her temper, sworn and shouted, and smacked them, but this happened only occasionally, once every four weeks, not on a daily basis. She had received little help from the father, as he was often out of the house working. She added that he had also shouted and screamed at them on occasions, but not as often. I wondered if she wanted any therapeutic help. She replied that she has calmed down now and did not want help. She had not thought of counselling or therapy, nor was she interested in the idea of getting help for herself.

OVERALL IMPRESSION

Overall, I had the impression of someone who clearly cared for her children and was very concerned about the current unusual and difficult situation. However, she was not someone with a great deal of insight into her own motivations. She did not understand why the children were behaving as they were, or why she had done nothing to obtain information about them from the school. I did not get the impression that there had been any major abuse of the children while they were in her care. She did agree that she had been excessively harsh at times, but not that often. I also had the impression that she was still very bitter about her ex-husband remarrying. What did concern me was the degree of perplexity and puzzlement she had about her current circumstances, as she did not seem to have much curiosity about her own contributions to the current problem

Interview with father

PRESENTING PROBLEMS

Father, in his late thirties, began his interview by talking about the children's point of view. He said they were well now, and that they did not know about the current proceedings in any detail. They were good, naughty at times like any children, but there were no signs of external distress, or any problems, and both were exceptionally clever. He explained how well they were doing at school, with their various achievements, and emphasized how happy they were. I asked him why they did not want to see their mother. He explained that they were happy in their current situation. They saw his wife as their mother figure. They were close to her and accepted love and discipline from her. She is cuddly and kisses them. Every two to three weeks he asked them if they wanted to see their mother, and he has explained that it would not upset him and his wife if they did; but they kept saying they did not want to and wondered why he kept asking.

I wondered if he had opinions about why things had reached this point. He said that he believed that things deteriorated some time after the birth of his daughter, when they began to quarrel a lot. He confirmed the mother's story about his staying out a lot to avoid her. But she gave the children to him at weekends, when he had to take over their care. She was also bad at disciplining them. She would shout and smack for no reason. She would blow up at the slightest incident, so that the children lost respect for her. She would frequently phone him at the office to ask for help. He said this as if it were a terrible thing to have done. I pointed out that she must have been desperate. He denied this. I added that she might well have been. He retorted that she had au pairs to help her. I tried to get him to see that she might have been desperate at that time, but he was reluctant to see that she had been helpless or needy in any way. He added that she resented the children with her at holiday time; she would do anything not to be with them. He felt now that around the time the children left her, if not before, there had been clear mental abuse, a view which he persisted in maintaining.

We went into the attempt to have contact at CAFCASS. He said dismissively that the professional dealing with this was an absolute disaster; she thought she was a child psychiatrist and could cure everybody. She had bullied him and threatened him into complying with her demands. The only reason that the children eventually went to the contact was that he forced them to go. He told them they had to go there and had no choice about it. I pointed out that this had probably not helped in that they were then bound to feel that the contact was going to be disastrous. However, he replied that if he had not said that they would never have got there at all. He did appear to be rather rigid, though he agreed that the meeting was doomed to fail if they had gone into it with that attitude. He added that the issue for him was if the children were happy, why disturb them?

He was still surprised about how adamant the children were about not wanting to see their mother. He thought that the situation would calm down after they came to live with him, but it had not. He could not understand this; though he did compare it to the fact that his ex- wife had fallen out with her own mother, whom she had not seen for many years. I certainly wondered myself, after he pointed it out, whether this was a major unconscious factor in the family dynamic—that when people fall out, they just do not see one another. Quite clearly, there was something powerful at work about a falling-out between parents and children.

FATHER'S BACKGROUND

The father talked warmly about his own family background. He was close to his mother, who was warm, caring, and loving, while his father was warm, caring, and gentle.

After the break-up of his marriage, the relationship with his ex-wife was good in that they communicated. But he felt that she was constantly denigrating him to the children, constantly poisoning them against him. She would also abuse him on the phone, and so he just got fed up with communicating with her. Every time he spoke to her he got a torrent of abuse. With regard to the school reports, he did not know whether or not she got them as he felt it was up to her to get them for herself. He felt that she did not really care for the children. She said she did, but in reality she did nothing to show she cared.

CONTACT ISSUES

I went into various issues about possible contact, and how it might be set up in a more neutral way, for example by him not taking the children himself. He did agree to this as a possibility and suggested a family member whom they knew might be a neutral person. He added that he was sceptical about this working as the mother had blown previous chances. For example, earlier on she had virtually ignored her son. However, the father was amenable to the idea of contact, if the children wished it, and he would do what he could to facilitate it.

OVERALL IMPRESSION

Overall, I had the impression that he was a caring parent, and also a very effective one. At the same time, he was clearly somewhat rigid in his attitudes and reluctant to see that his ex-wife might have been vulnerable in the past, and possibly still so in the present. Essentially, he had dismissed her from his mind, rather as the children seemed to have done.

He had a lot of righteous anger about his ex-wife, which was difficult to shift. At the same time, he might have had a point about her excessive anger, and I also did believe that he had tried to encourage the children to see their mother. I did not get the impression that he was trying to brainwash them, though it was likely that he did not want his ex-wife to interfere with what appeared to be a happy family life, and that this was communicated to his children.

INTERVIEW WITH BOTH PARENTS

I next thought it was worth trying to see whether or not it was feasible to negotiate a new arrangement with *both* parents together. However, this negotiation was not possible. It was a very difficult and tense meeting, in which the breakdown of the relationship between the parents was very tangible, and it was not possible to find any compromise. The father still felt she had abused the children, and the mother denied that she had. I did push the father quite considerably to acknowledge that she might have been vulnerable, but he maintained his position that she just had not cared enough.

When we talked about possible neutral contact arrangements, the mother suggested a family member whom the children had not seen for years. This clearly indicated an unrealistic attitude to a very complex situation, but she did agree to the father's suggested family member.

We did agree that there may be an explanation for the children's behaviour in terms of one or more of the following possibilities.

First, that their attitude had become a way of life, as it were, because they were settled in their new home and did not want to be reminded of the past. Second, what they said about the harshness with which they had been treated might simply be true and they did not want to be reminded of it. Third, there might be complex family dynamics involved, for example about children and parents falling out.

At the end, the father agreed to bring both children to see me individually, in order to attempt to ascertain their own wishes, and we also agreed on a provisional time for the contact should they wish it.

Interview with children

I first saw the children together with their father for a brief introduction to my assessment. They both knew why they had come. They said it was to do with their mother. The father explained that both of them had not wanted to come as they felt it was a waste of time, but he that he had tried to tell them to keep an open mind. I pointed out that I was not there to change their mind necessarily, but to see what they wished and then to see what was best for them.

In the detailed interviews with me both children separately maintained that their life was happy now, unlike before when they were living with their mother, and that they did not want to see her. Even when I clarified that there was not an issue about them returning to live with her, which they might have feared, they still maintained their position. They did not want to be reminded of their past bad experiences.

The boy did not dwell much on the past, though the girl was still preoccupied by memories of being bullied by her mother and fears that she would come and take her away from her father.

When asked for specific details of what their mother did to them, the boy talked about her punishing them for no good reason, unlike the father, who told him off only when he deserved it. He could not recall any happy times with her, and he was adamant that the father had not insisted that he did not see his mother; on the contrary, he said that his father had tried hard to persuade him to have contact with her, but he was adamant that he did not want this. He was still afraid of being hit by her for no reason.

The girl also described being punished unfairly. The mother did not hit them the whole time, but they were often put into their rooms for no good reason. She did not want to see her mother even if the contact were supervised. She did not want to feel uncomfortable again, and she was afraid of becoming miserable again. She was very fond of her stepmother, who was warm and played a lot with them. She never lost her temper like her mother. Sometimes at night she thought about what her mother did to them, and then she couldn't go to sleep, but this happened less often now.

Conclusions

Quite clearly, both children were adamant that they did not want contact with their mother. They had a stable and happy home life and did not want to be reminded of their unhappy past. This was a very sad situation, but I did not see a way of forcing them to have direct contact with their mother. This had been tried and had failed dismally. The children were perhaps too anxious that their current family life would be unduly disturbed by being reminded of past unhappiness. One could not completely rule out the possibility that they had been unduly influenced by their father's scornful attitude to his ex-wife, but overall they seemed clear about their own views.

The reports from CAFCASS confirmed my own findings. The Children and Family Reporter had the impression that the mother had felt unsupported in bringing up the children during her marriage, but she also had the impression that she had over-chastised the children. In her interview with the father he made the point that if his ex-wife had accepted responsibility for the way she had made the children feel, then they would have wanted to see her.

I thought this was a valid point in that it related to my own interview with her when she showed that she found it difficult to accept responsibility and had little insight into her own difficulties. During the Children Reporter's interviews with the children, she did not get the impression that they were frightened by their mother, but it seemed that they had been severely punished by her. Meanwhile, they had formed a strong bond with their stepmother, to the point where they had rejected their mother. During my interview with the mother, she felt that her disciplining of them was normal and felt that they had exaggerated her handling of them. I did think that, whether or not this were true, if a parent found themselves in this unfortunate situation where their children did not want to see them, they would have to re-examine their whole attitude and begin to think that they may have done something untoward. The mother maintained that she had done nothing wrong.

When seen together, both mother and father found it difficult to communicate with one another; mother suspected that father had turned the children against her, while father found it difficult to see her vulnerability.

In conclusion, my opinion was that it seemed at that moment impossible to persuade either child to attempt to renew contact with their mother. This was a very sad situation, but it did seem pretty clear that they did not wish contact for the moment and for the foreseeable future. They both felt that their lives were happy now, and they did not wish to be reminded of their past unhappiness with their mother. While this was an unusual and rather a worrying situation, I thought that any attempt to force the children to see their mother again would be doomed to fail, and would not be in their interests.

I suspected that the best option at that moment was to maintain indirect contact, and to make sure the father provided regular updates on the children's progress. The children, in the meantime, should be left alone, so that they could come to think about seeing their mother again in their own time. I did not see any clear evidence that the father was putting undue pressure on the children.

While the mother did not subject them to major and significant harm, what both children described was the use of undue punishment, threatened or otherwise, and an ongoing atmosphere of injustice. While to an outsider the kind of disciplining used by the mother may seem unwise and inappropriate, it hardly appeared to be cruel or significantly abusive. None the less, in the children's minds, particularly now that they were settled and happy in their new home, life with their mother appeared unacceptably harsh. They both felt that she had not provided proper parenting for them, and that they received this in their new home. Thus, I felt that there was no option but to accept the children's point of view. I hoped that maintaining effective indirect contact would ultimately have a beneficial effect in allowing the children to rethink their position. Anything else at that moment would simply force them to be even more intransigent.

Example three: intransigent parent

BACKGROUND

I was asked to give an opinion about whether or not a father should have direct contact with his two children, a young teenage girl and her younger brother. In the joint letter of instruction, I was informed that the parents had separated some three years previously, and that the mother had left the home with the children. Since then the father had seen the children on only a few occasions. The mother had alleged that the relationship with her ex-husband had been violent, which he denied. She also alleged that the children did not wish to see their father, although the children had given contrary views in the past to the Children's Reporter I was asked to deal with the following issues:

1.   The relationship of the children with their parents.
2.   The relationship between the parties and the level of hostility.
3.   The impact of alleged domestic violence on their relationship.
4.   Recommendations in respect of contact—direct or indirect, immediate or future.

5.   Recommendations as to priorities in respect of therapeutic treatment for the family as a whole or for individual members.

In view of the breakdown in communication between the parents and, apparently, between the father and the children, I decided to see the father and then the mother with the children separately, before deciding whether or not to see the parents together, and/or the father and the children.

Interview with father

I spent some two hours interviewing the father. Although he was pleasant and cooperative it was quite difficult to tie him down to specific details, as he tended to go into rather long stories when I asked him any question. It was thus difficult to obtain a focused picture of himself and his background. In the end, I just described what took place.

PRESENTING PROBLEMS

When I asked the father what the current situation was, he replied that it was bloody pointless and stupid in his view. He had been told through a lawyer's letter that unless he agreed to anger management training he would not be able to see his children. He had also been warned that he had to grovel if he wanted to see them. But he would not grovel to anyone.

This became a main theme of the meeting. He came across as an independent and proud man, who, as he put it to me, would not do what people told him to do. If he chose to do something then he would do it; but if he were ordered to get help there was no way that he would comply. It was very difficult to find middle ground with him. He tended to see things in extremes and also had great difficulty in seeing other people's points of view. This stubborn intransigence had not helped him in trying to deal with a complicated situation with regard to his own children.

He had last seen the children at a contact centre some two years previously. The first occasion was fine, but at the second meeting only his son came, and he was told his daughter was sick and was afraid of seeing him. However, then she turned up. He did not want to talk to her as she was grinning at him. He then gave her a sealed envelope addressed to her mother, which said not to be opened unless something happened to him. He explained that this was a copy of his will, in which he had left everything to his children. I was feeling that this was a strange thing to be doing via a contact visit, but he felt this was quite all right. He then began to reveal a lot of anger and grievance about his situation, although he never lost control in the interview.

The father complained that he had written many letters to the children but had hardly had any in reply, because of their mother's influence. While he was upset by this he added that he was not allowed by the court to be upset as it would show he was an unsuitable parent. He then described how close he had been to his children; for example, how often he would take them places. But they had been snatched from him.

MARITAL RELATIONSHIP

While they got on well from the start, he said that his wife was always very jealous. When he was away on business, or occasionally playing cards with friends all night, she would think he was with another woman. He described how once when she was pregnant and they were on holiday, he went to have a drink on his own. She did not come because she was tired and had told him to enjoy himself. So he had dinner on his own, went to a club for a drink, and next went to a casino, and then came back to the hotel in the early morning. She gave him grief for being out so late and accused him of being with another woman. That was typical, he added.

On several occasions he told me stories about the stress he had to put up with, after which he would have a drink to calm down. I certainly got the impression that at the very least drink figured largely in his life. There was also a brush with the police following a row at home. She had called the police, and when they came to talk to him he had told them to piss off, so he ended up in a cell. He was only released after he had agreed to take a caution. But he only did this after a policeman had agreed to give him a cup of coffee first. He had decided that if he had been refused the coffee, he would not then have budged.

This kind of attitude was typical of several stories he told me about his involvement with others. Conditions and a degree of control were often put forward by him before he would agree to cooperate. When I pointed this out to him, he saw absolutely nothing wrong in it.

When I asked him what led to the breakdown of his marriage, he found it difficult to be precise. He said that he had been very happy in the marriage, and he showed me photos of his ex-wife. He added that she did not leave because of being unhappy. He was not aware of things breaking down. I said that must have been a problem. He replied by telling me another complicated story about a car being the excuse, which I simply could not follow. There was something about him feeling undermined as the authority of the household. I wondered if he were too concerned about his own authority. He said no. He gave me another story about her jealousy, but denied any jealousy himself. I wondered if he kept feelings to himself, to which I got no clear response. I had the impression that he was reluctant to look at his own responsibility for what may have happened in the marriage. He kept blaming his ex-wife for being too jealous and for not respecting him enough.

FAMILY BACKGROUND

His own upbringing, from a large family, was strict and at times quite punitive, though he defended it as good for him. He gave a number of vivid examples to illustrate what he meant. With his own children he was also strict, though not as much as his parents had been with him. He told them not to tell lies, and he rarely smacked them—which was confirmed later by his ex-wife. He denied any violence towards his wife—though her story was different. He would not talk about his father, who had died some years before. But he did tell me that his mother was easy-going but was also used to putting her foot down when necessary.

CONTACT ISSUES

Towards the end of the meeting, I asked him what he would like to happen. He said he wanted free and realistic access to his children. He would be prepared to see his ex-wife to talk about this; he has offered to do so several times, but there had been no reply. He felt she was using the children to get at him. They had been poisoned by her. If there were direct contact, he would agree to it being supervised, provided she was not there I asked him if he would be able to keep his feelings about her to himself if he saw the children again. He replied dismissively, if unconvincingly, that he was not interested in her and would not waste time talking about her.

I ended by describing how I intended going about the rest of the assessment, and that I would clearly need to see both children on their own. He said that if that were the case I would have to get permission from the court because the mother would not let them see me. In fact, it turned out that there was no problem at all with her letting me see the children; on the contrary, she facilitated this.

OVERALL IMPRESSION

My overall impression of the father was that he was someone who cared deeply about his children and would very much like to have direct contact with them. He felt aggrieved about what had happened, and felt that it was unjust that he had hardly any indirect communication with the children. He blamed his wife for all of this, omitting any responsibility for his own behaviour, including a significant number of quite inappropriate remarks made in letters to the children about his views of their mother, copies of which I had already been given. He blamed her jealousy for what had gone wrong in their relationship. He was someone who was independent and private, and also, as he put it himself, autocratic. He was not someone who found it easy to compromise, because, as he also put it, his strict upbringing had taught him right and wrong. Rather than see any middle ground, he would take one side and then find it difficult to shift, because to do so would feel like a humiliation.

Interview with mother and children

PRESENTING PROBLEMS

I saw the mother and children together for a while, and asked what the children understood about coming to see me. The girl understood very well the nature of the interviews, but the boy was somewhat tense and clung to his mother for a while, though he gradually relaxed. They gave me a picture of a settled and happy family life. The girl was outgoing and confident, while the boy was rather more anxious. I asked the mother if there were any worries about the children. She said no, apart from a recent incident involving their father, when he sat outside their new house in his car, even though he was allowed contact, and the children were a little upset about this. She added that she and their father do not meet; they meet separately with teachers at school. The girl added that she did not want to see her father because she felt happy with the way things were. She did not want to start things over again at the contact centre.

At that point she began to look upset. Mother explained that she herself had tried to encourage the children to give their father a chance. She did pass his letters on to them. They were quite inappropriate at first, and this concerned her. She felt she shouldn't give these things to the children, so she would read the letters first to make sure they were appropriate before passing them on. She did her best to encourage them to write to him, but they were reluctant to do so. She also made it clear to the children that they could talk to me and say whatever they wanted to.

Interview with mother

After organizing some toys and activities to be available for the children in the waiting room, I interviewed the mother.

First of all, I wondered where she was in herself. She replied that she was a different person. She used to be on the edge the whole time, constantly anxious when with her ex-husband. He used to like his drink, and she never knew what mood he would be in. He was also physically violent to her, including slapping her face, pushing her, putting his hands round her neck, and also using verbal abuse—none of which he had admitted to me. I wondered when this happened. She said that after work he would go the pub before coming home. The drink was the main reason for the violence. He had always been masterful and domineering, and what he said had to go. He was difficult to negotiate with and he had never listened to her point of view. With regard to the violence, I established that she had never gone to casualty, and it was only slaps across the face. Once a row had escalated and he had grabbed her round the neck. He was like Jekyll and Hyde—one moment he could be charming, especially to outsiders, a real diamond; but once inside the house, he would be different, a tyrant.

He did love the children, but he was difficult with them. For example, he would often tell them to be quiet while he watched sport on television. The boy might be running a car across the carpet and the father would tell him to do that somewhere else. The children were not allowed to cry, as his family did not show their tears. He was a very private person, autocratic and a disciplinarian; it was difficult to get to the real him—which matched my own impression.

He occasionally took the children out at weekends. She then described one incident when he left his son in the care of his daughter while he went to a pub. But then the son got lost for a while and the father told the girl not to tell his wife. In general, he rarely had the children on his own.

MARITAL RELATIONSHIP

We went into the early years of their relationship. It seemed that all was well until she became pregnant, when he began to go off her. He explained that he did not like the sight of pregnant women, and he began to stay out more and more. She felt very unsupported, but denied being jealous. She never wondered what he was up to because he always came back. On specific questioning, she denied being a jealous person. One could thus see a marked discrepancy between their two stories—he said she was jealous, she said he was unsupportive.

FAMILY BACKGROUND

Her own childhood was happy, with a supportive family. Both parents were described as loving and caring. Her pregnancies were normal, though somewhat emotionally difficult. When her daughter was due to be born, her ex-husband took her to the hospital, but was not involved during the birth. When she was born, he showed no enthusiasm for her being a girl, and she did not see him for a day. That was a typical pattern; he turned up his nose at whatever did not suit him. He was more enthusiastic when his son was born.

CONTACT ISSUES

When we went into the contact issues, she described that she had tried to encourage them to go, but did not insist, as they were not at all keen about them. She described how her daughter had told her that he constantly questioned her about what she was up to, her boyfriends, etc., in a very intrusive way. Because of that kind of behaviour, and because the children were now happy, she felt that the children were not ready for contact. Her son had virtually to be forced to go. She added that if the children had been happy to see their father, she would go along with it. She said she would be concerned, but would try to support it, and that it would preferably take place in a contact centre. She also described the inappropriate letters he often sent, including the episode with the will, which upset the children.

OVERALL IMPRESSION

In general, I had the impression of a woman who had found a new life for herself and her children, which was, from her description and from what I later saw from the children, clearly a happy and settled life. I had the impression that she had tried to encourage the children to reply to their father's letters and had tried to encourage contact. She did not actively denigrate her ex-husband, but had a pretty realistic view of his rigid personality. I felt that she was reluctant for him to have direct contact because she was genuinely worried about the effect on the children.

INTERVIEWS WITH CHILDREN

I saw each child individually.

The girl was bright and mature. She was able to talk about herself and I felt she understood the current situation well. I asked her about her school, which she clearly enjoyed, then about a typical day at home, where she appeared happy. I asked her to describe her mother, whom she said was friendly, understanding, and helpful to her and her brother. She and her brother did things together, and he often made her laugh. When I asked her about her father, she said that he used to say horrible stuff to her about her mother. She recalled hearing them argue a lot. Her father would come in late from the pub and she would go downstairs to listen to the arguments. He never hit her or her brother, though he once got her mother by the neck. I asked whether he did things with them. She said that when she was seven or eight they would go to the park on their bikes, but this was only occasionally, and they never played together.

I asked what she felt about seeing her father again for contact. Her reply at first was not at the moment as she was happy as she was. Then she added that maybe she would once in a while, but only for an hour. I tried to get an idea of how often this would be, so gave her various options. The only time that was acceptable to her was once every two months or so. She was clear that she did not want to see him regularly, and only very occasionally at the most. Her main worry that this would lead on to more contact. She was not afraid that she might lose her mother, only that her father would think he could then see them more often. I tried to clarify if this opinion was as a result of her mother's influence; but she was absolutely clear that her view came form inside her, and, if anything, her mother had tried to encourage her to go to the contact.

It was my view that the girl was speaking honestly about something that she herself felt. I made it clear that I would take her views seriously when I came to my own recommendations. I also told her that whatever was decided now, when she was a little older she could make up her own mind about what, if any, contact she could have.

When I saw the boy, his main worry was that if he saw his father he would lose his mother. I asked him if this was what his mother had told him or what he felt inside, and he said it was what he felt inside. It was difficult to know exactly how to make sense of what he was telling me because of his overwhelming fear. I felt that, unlike him, his sister was mature enough to be able to know what she felt about the situation.

I had a final interview with the mother to confirm some of the details of the interviews, and also to find out whether or not she would agree to a meeting with her ex-husband, which she was not keen on, in view of his bullying attitude.

Documents

In my comments about the various papers and previous reports, I noted a number of inappropriate comments made to the children in letters sent to them by the father. For example, he talked about writing to solicitors, about invasion of his privacy, and once about some people who had died. These sorts of comment probably made it difficult to take on board some other more encouraging comments about, for example, their school progress. He seemed to have little idea about how to be child focused.

In the Children's Reporter's report the father denied allegations of domestic violence, though he did own up to shaking his ex-wife in the past, and also to shouting at her and calling her names. The children at that time, some two years previously, also talked about their parents' arguments, but they could also recall happier times. They also described how their father did not like their friends coming round to play because of the noise; he did not like his peace to be disturbed.

Contact at that time was taking place, even though it was fraught at times, with the father giving the mother unpleasant looks, and on one occasion becoming openly angry with her about some school report. The reports commented that he did not realize how intimidating he could be. The situation then escalated, with the father demanding from his daughter information, such as where they lived, and making intrusive comments about their life with their mother. The father was unable to control the bitterness he felt towards his ex-wife in the children's presence, making contact very uncomfortable. At the same time he was unable or unwilling to concede that there was anything wrong with his behaviour, nor did he agree to have meetings to discuss his attitude with the Children's Reporter, or with anyone else.

The papers revealed that there had been no shift in the situation prior to my assessment. The father continued to blame the mother for turning the children against him, and his attitude was that he was not to blame for what had gone wrong in the past. He also took no responsibility for his inappropriate behaviour, and he considered that comments about what he had written in the letters to his children were an invasion of his privacy. This rigid attitude essentially made it difficult to resolve the situation. One could thus understand the mother's reluctance for the resumption of direct contact with the children. On the other hand, the children still loved him and there were indications that they wanted some kind of direct contact, even if it were of a minimal kind.

Conclusions

In the conclusion to my report, I began by outlining the basic principles of contact, as outlined at the beginning of the chapter.

Essentially, direct contact should be in the best interest of the child, even where there may have been some intimidation or harassment. The issue with this family seemed not that clear-cut, in that the harassment and/or violence had not been as extreme as one sees in a number of other cases, where there is clear evidence of major violent incidents, including visits to casualty departments, broken bones, and criminal charges. In those circumstances, it was easier to make decisions about limiting contact. But in this situation, the level of intimidation appeared to be less severe, even if everything the mother had described about her experiences were true.

On the other hand, one could not underestimate the effect on children of witnessing marital violence and discord. There was clear evidence, both from previous reports and from my own interviews, that the children were afraid of their father, and it was my view that this fear was not fostered by the mother; it came genuinely from them. There was also clear evidence from the letters that the father did not have a consistently good idea of what was appropriate to put in a letter to the children, but nor did he agree to accept any advice about this or any other matter related to the children.

I did not feel that the children would be at risk of suffering physical harm were they to have supervised access to their father, though I thought that there was still the possibility of him harassing them, or putting undue and inappropriate pressure on them again. He continued to have difficulty in seeing their point of view, and I thought that this needed to change before the situation could move on. Clearly, the children had been affected by the family circumstances, the fact that there had been a separation, that they had witnessed arguments between the parents, and the fact that there was no agreement between the parents about contact. Despite this, the children appeared to be leading a stable and happy life. One of the issues was whether or not one should disturb this stability for the father's sake at that moment, because in the long term it would be in the children's interests to have some contact with their father.

Although there was some evidence that the father wished contact in order to promote the children's interests, for example by also having contact with his family, there was other evidence that his desire to have contact was also a means of continuing his dispute with his ex-wife, whom he still had not forgiven for daring to leave him. In addition, he had continued to fail to acknowledge his own contribution to what had happened. He had reluctantly agreed that he was autocratic, but as far as having other weaknesses, he maintained a position of merely being wronged. He also showed little or no capacity to change. He tended to take rather stubborn and fixed attitudes because of his own sense of injustice, and because he felt that he had to be in the right. He gave me the impression that it would be utterly humiliating for him to back down, as he would feel as if he were being treated like a child.

I was asked to deal with a number of specific questions.

Question one asked about the relationship between the parents and the children, and I answered that brother and sister seemed to have a good relationship with their mother, whom they obviously trusted and were happy with. I did not observe the children with their father, as I felt it was inappropriate at that point, given the children's anxieties about him. I suggested that one could describe their relationship with him at that time as tentative and cautious.

In the second question I was asked about the relationship between the parents and the level of any hostility. Quite clearly, there was an ongoing and long-standing breakdown of their relationship, which made it difficult to negotiate an acceptable arrangement for the children.

The third question concerned the impact of alleged domestic violence on the parental relationship. I replied that, if the alleged violence were found to have taken place, then it would have been a major contribution to the breakdown of their relationship, particularly if the father denied it and, in addition, denied his excessive drinking.

I then came to my main recommendations about contact.

First, I made a clear recommendation that there should not be regular direct contact at that moment. In summary, the reasons for this were that the children, particularly the girl, did not wish this, and she made this wish plain. I argued that regular direct contact would increase the children's anxieties, given their own concerns about what it would be like, where it would lead, and the fact that there had not been contact for some time. It was my view that it would thus be unwise to move quickly to regular direct contact.

My second recommendation was that there should be indirect contact, including letters and photos. However, it was clear at that time that the father's letters would need to be monitored, in view of their occasional inappropriate contents.

There remained the issue of infrequent direct contact, of the order of every two months or so in the first place. I suggested that there were arguments for and against this.

The arguments in favour of such contact were that the children did have a father, whom they had a right to know, even if there were current difficulties about this. The girl had indicated some wish to see him, albeit not a strong wish at that time. In principle, it is in children's interests to see their father, and, indeed, I considered that it would be in these children's interests to have direct contact with him, provided it could be managed in a safe and contained way.

Arguments against infrequent direct contact were the fact that the father had yet to prove that he could manage contact in a child-appropriate way. I was unsure about the wisdom of proceeding with such direct contact without prior preparation of the children and prior work with the father.

I was asked to comment on recommendations as to any therapeutic treatment for the family as a whole, or for individual members. I did not get the impression that the mother or the children needed therapeutic work at that time. However, I certainly did believe that the father would benefit from some short-term counselling focused on changing his attitude towards the children. I thought that he needed to understand that his own behaviour had an impact on the children, and that he needed to contain himself in their presence. However, I was pessimistic about him accepting any help. He had made it clear that this would be humiliating, that he did not, as he put it, like being treated like a child, and he considered that he was in the right. This made any attempt to get him to shift his position particularly difficult, as it would feel to him like a complete shift in world view. None the less, I did feel it was important for him to accept some meetings centred around how to make his communications more child focused, and I even offered to do them myself if necessary.

Court hearing

Because my recommendations were not accepted by the father, a court hearing to decide the issue of contact took place. The

Children's Reporter and I were in agreement about our recommendations, and this was put to the parties before going into court. The father's barrister tried to persuade him to agree to the recommendations, but he would not be budged. He stuck to his view that he was right and everyone else was wrong, and he would not accept any form of help, preparation, or counselling, whether that were anger management or anything else.

When I gave my own evidence, the issue of the father's extended family came up as a possible neutral place where the children could at least have some contact with the father, even if it were only through his family connections, and this seemed a good idea. But anything else was effectively ruled out. In the end, the judge ruled that there should only be indirect contact, and that other options would have to wait for the foreseeable future, and were dependent on the children's wishes.

Example four: depressed parent

BACKGROUND

Mrs T's lawyer instructed me to assess her mental health in order to see whether or not she could resume some care of her two children, a boy aged ten and a girl aged eight, following a period when she left them in the care of their father. The letter of instruction was not very full, nor were there many documents available, though there was a report from a Children's Reporter who had seen the children, as well as witness statements from both parents. I was given permission to obtain medical records from the mother's GP, but they never arrived, despite my requesting them several times. I was not allowed to see the children, or their father. Thus, I had to give an opinion about a difficult situation as a result of seeing only the mother and having limited information, which obviously restricted my view of this situation.

Interview with mother

PRESENTING PROBLEMS

I saw the mother for some two hours, and felt that I had got to know her reasonably well. She had a history of depression, which had come on gradually over the period of her marriage, and which had not been treated effectively. There was also a clear family history of depression. Her illness, which went unrecognized both by the husband and by her then GP, eventually led to her abandoning the children, moving away from them for some time, until she eventually recovered. By the time I saw her, she had got her life together again, was no longer depressed, and wished to resume some care of the children. However, her ex-husband absolutely refused to countenance such a move, on the basis that she was unstable, inconsistent, and had walked out on the children.

I was asked to determine whether or not Mrs T had had post natal depression, which could account for her behaviour. It was in fact difficult to be precise about this, for though the mother said first of all that she had post natal depression after the birth of her children, this was not clear when I went over the details of the birth of the children. Unfortunately, her medical records were never sent to me, and so the issue of post natal depression was unclear. The depression in fact seemed to be more related to long-standing marital difficulties, to her feeling unsupported by her husband, and by the shock of leaving her work and having to look after the children full-time. In addition, there was the contribution of the family history, with her mother and other family members suffering from long-standing depression. Her own family was not one where it was possible to talk much about feelings; they were just blotted out. As she put it, they played at happy families.

MARITAL RELATIONSHIP

Mrs T said that her marriage had been happy initially, but that things began to deteriorate when they moved out of the city where they had first settled. Her husband would commute, often leaving her alone for long periods. The birth of her first child was normal, but after about six months or so, she began to feel increasingly cut off. Her second child's birth was a traumatic forceps delivery. Although her daughter's development was normal, the girl cried a lot and would not be comforted. Mrs T increasingly felt desperate about her situation, her difficulty in coping with the day to day care of the children, while her husband would never talk to her. He just assumed she would cope and could not see how vulnerable she was. His attitude was that they had a nanny, so why was she complaining. In fact, the nanny's competence only made her feel even more inadequate. She could not talk to girl friends. In fact, she had an enormous fear of depression and of losing control, like her own mother had experienced when she was a child.

HER DEPRESSION

She went to her GP on a number of occasions but never received any help. She was told that she was feeling like that because she had two young children to look after and that she just needed a holiday. She had increasing insomnia, began putting on weight, and her already poor self image worsened. She also felt that she could never live up to her husband's high expectations, and she felt increasingly undermined by his criticisms. She would lose her temper with the children and that made her feel like her own mother, and also made her believe that she was a bad mother. This in itself was like a vicious circle and made matters even worse.

Mrs T had nihilistic and suicidal thoughts for some two years, still without help. In retrospect, it was clear that she was suffering from a severe depression. It was a tragedy that she was not offered appropriate help, which might have forestalled her subsequent action. But she also did not reveal to her doctor the extent of her suicidalness. Eventually, she decided to leave the home, for she felt that if she didn't she would kill herself.

She did not take the children as she felt she was in no fit state to look after them. She lived with friends for a while; there were brief but unsuccessful attempts at reconciliation, and she moved out permanently. Her whole world had fallen apart. After a turbulent period of time, including unsatisfactory brief relationships, she began to sort herself out. A new GP was very supportive, prescribed antidepressants, and helped her become stable again. It was for that reason that she now wanted to have joint care of the children. She explained that they also wanted to see more of her now. However, her ex-husband, who was in a new relationship, was totally against this. He was still angry about her leaving the children in his care. In his view, the children were happy and settled, and should not be put through any more suffering. There was no acknowledgement that Mrs T might have been suffering from depression, or that he had failed to pick up how depressed she was while they were together.

Documents

There was one rather brief report from a Court Welfare Officer, which described how both children were suffering from the parental conflicts, as well as the effect of their mother's breakdown. But there were no clear recommendations, and no follow-up.

Overall impression

My own interview with the mother clearly revealed a history of untreated depression, which probably explained why she eventually ended up leaving her children. It was, she put it, either that or killing herself. She was driven to leave the home for fear of emotionally damaging her children. However, it was also reasonably clear, as far as I could see, that her depression was better and that she had built up a more stable life. While her predisposition to depression might remain, there had been no recurrence, and the major external factors which had led to her severe depressive illness had been removed, namely her social isolation, the pressures of looking after young children on a day-to-day basis with a husband who expected her to cope no matter what.

I thought it would be helpful for Mrs T to have formal psychotherapy, and she was certainly interested in this option. However, she also explained that she had looked for counselling recently, but her ex-husband's lawyer had used this as another reason for her not to have any care of the children—an appalling, but unfortunately not uncommon tactic. It was difficult for me to make strong recommendations, given the fact that I had not seen the father or the children. My offer to do so was not taken up. However, I did suggest that joint residency be considered as a feasible option. This was not a situation where there was no contact; on the contrary, both parties were agreeable to contact. The question was whether or not it was in the children's best interests to change their current circumstances. I thought that it would be unwise to make a major change in their circumstances, given the fact that they had stability in their life thanks to their father. He might or might not be the best person to be in touch with their feelings. I could not comment on this without seeing him with the children. At the same time, it was in the children's interests to maintain contact with their mother, and to have increased contact if they expressed a wish to have this.

The ideal arrangement would have been for both parties to agree without having to pursue the matter in court. In that way, the children's anxieties about their parents' dispute would be diminished. The father's main point was that he did not believe that the mother was sufficiently stable to resume the burden of motherhood, or having the children to stay for any length of time. While I agreed that it would be unwise simply to return the children to her, I could not see that having depression in the past, even with the mother's predisposition, should prevent her from sharing some of the parenting, particularly as the children were older.

Outcome of situation

I was never directly informed about what the court decided. I was never called to give evidence, nor was I asked to do any further assessment of the family members. Out of interest I wrote to the solicitor a year or so later to ask what happened, and to my surprise, he replied that unfortunately, as a result of my report, mother's counsel had advised that she drop the application for joint residency, and so the situation was unchanged.

Example five: vulnerable children

BACKGROUND

I was asked to comment on contact arrangements between a mentally ill mother and her two boys, aged nine and seven, who were living permanently with the mother's sister. The mother had fortnightly contact with the children, but at the time of the original instructions she was asking for more frequent contact, and the relationship between her and the aunt had deteriorated.

There had been a previous history of the mother not maintaining contact, for a variety of reasons, both during recurrence of her severe depressions, and because of her chaotic life style. However, by the time I saw the aunt, the boys and the mother, the situation had improved. The mother no longer wanted increased contact; she had kept to contact arrangements for the previous months, and the sisters were talking to one another. Despite the improvement, the parties wished me to see the family in case the situation deteriorated again, and because there were concerns about the older boy, whose behaviour was rapidly deteriorating and who was apparently receiving little help from his local services.

My assessment lasted just over three hours and consisted of interviews with the aunt and the boys both together and individually, and then the mother with the boys and on her own.

Interviews with aunt and children

The aunt and the children arrived on time, accompanied by someone from her lawyer's office in order to help look after the children during the interviews, and came up to my room.

I asked her if the children knew why they were coming and why she had come herself, and she explained that it was to do with how the children felt about things and how it affects them, as well as issues of contact with their mother. The children had lived with their aunt for most of their lives and permanently for the past five years. Quite clearly she was effectively their mother and both children were happy with her. She said that most of the time at the moment things were fine. Their mother's unsupervised contact had been kept up regularly for the last nine months. This was the longest period of regular contact, every other weekend for a few hours. It usually went well, though the children did play up a bit when they came home. They would start arguing, fighting, and hurting each other until bedtime, then they usually settled down. I asked her what her view was about increasing contact. She said that in principle she had no objection, but she doubted whether the mother could maintain this. In the past there had been problems when mother cancelled contact at the last minute, causing the children grief.

The main problem at the moment was the behaviour of the nine year old, "Steven". He had just been excluded from school because of violence and disruptive behaviour. He had been violent towards children and teachers and had wrecked a classroom. After several suspensions he had now been excluded. She did not know why this had happened. He had had numerous behavioural problems; he had wrecked the house, had violent tantrums with other children, and he had once threatened her with a carving knife.

Around this time, the two boys started to wind one another up. They quarrelled over what animal in my toy box they would each play with, The aunt had to be very firm about sharing, and they calmed down. In fact, it was the younger boy, "Simon" who did the winding up, while Steven was quite calm. It was only later in the morning that he revealed his potential for violence.

I wondered what plans there were for Steven. She said there were none. At times she felt at the end of her tether. Nothing was sorted out for Steven; he needed to be statemented, but that had not gone ahead. There was no appointment for the local Child Psychiatry clinic. The whole situation with him seemed very worrying, with little or no clear strategy for helping him. The aunt added that Simon could be aggravating at times, but otherwise he was not a problem at school, and his progress was satisfactory.

I asked her to describe a typical day. She said that they got up for school. This was reasonably easy most days, unless Steven was refusing, and then he would throw a tantrum—crashing and banging around and refusing to go to school. A lot of the time she ignored it, although she would intervene if he became too violent and then sit him down. In fact, she had tried every possible behavioural technique with him without much success. He did go to foster parents to give her a break every fortnight. He then said "I don't have to go!", and she replied that he did. I wondered with them how we could understand his disruptive behaviour. She thought it had a lot to do with what happened to the boys in the past, but then she would have hoped they would have settled down. There had been a lot of uncertainty in their lives, with their parents coming and going, breaking up and coming together, and leaving them at various points. She thought that a lot of it was about the boys not understanding what was happening to them early in their life. The children listened to her explanation, and then I saw each child in turn, starting with the younger boy, Simon.

Interview with Simon

He was playing with the animals in an enclosure he had created. There was a person in a car who then caught the animals; he owned a zoo, and all the animals had escaped before he caught them. He liked zoos. He also liked playing with action figures, for example from *Star Wars*, and Micro machines. He said he liked playing at home with his computer. His favourite television programmes were *Pokemon*, and *The Simpsons*. He liked collecting Pokemon cards, and he had loads of them. He had friends, and went round to their houses, and they came to his house, and they played on computers. He had a special friend, whom he named. He saw him a lot. He also played with four or five special friends at school. His favourite subject was science, and his least favourite maths. English was OK, although he had difficulty spelling some of the words, and his writing was not neat. I wondered if he made up stories. He told me one about a man digging a coal mine who found some eggs, and a monster came out of them. The monster ate a man and took over the world, but a boy came and destroyed them with his brother. He smiled when I made a comment that his story might have something to do with himself having to deal with monsters and things that worried him.

This led on to his talking specifically about his worries. He was worried about what Steven was up to. He could be threatening with a knife, and he also ran away from home and could get in a strop. He was also worried about his mum being OK as she was ill. She lived with his Nan and she took pills and was getting better now. I asked what they did when they saw their mother. He replied that they played with her and talked. For example, she would say where do you want to go, and what presents did you get at Easter, etc. And then she would talk to Steven, while he went into another room. She would talk to him about his bad behaviour. I wondered why he thought his behaviour was so difficult, and Simon said he did not know.

Simon slept well, and had no bad dreams, though he used to have one about a monster eating him. I asked him specifically about contact again, and he said that things were fine, maybe he could do with a little more of it, but there was no strong indication of his wanting a change. We also talked a little about the extended family and also his aunt, with whom he was happy. She was sometimes a little angry when they fought, but otherwise very kind. She made good dinners and he was very happy with her. Finally, I asked him if he wanted to chat to anybody about any worries he had, and he said he did not know.

Overall, I had the impression of a fairly normal boy who was reasonably able to talk about himself. He had concerns about his mother's illness but he did seem in general to be developing satisfactorily.

Interview with Steven

He began by telling me about the asthma he had had for the last two years. He had to have inhalers and tablets. He showed me his Pokemon watch, which he had been given as a present. He also collected the cards. I wondered what he liked to do. He said anything artistic, like drawing. He also liked making things. He had made a scarecrow, which he would have shown me if he could have brought it. I thought that it was most interesting that this apparently disturbed boy wanted to show me his creative side at the beginning of the interview, and it was noticeable how contained he was at first. I wondered with him that, in view of what he was telling me, why was it he also wanted to break things. He said he did not know. It was not feelings coming up, though he did get angry. Simon aggravated him and wound him up—as in fact I had already seen. I asked him what else made him angry. He replied that when someone said no to him, or tried to stop him, or wanted him to do something he did not want to do. Thus, he was easily frustrated.

I asked him about his earliest memory. He said he remembered quite a lot, and he described an early scene when his parents were together and were travelling around and he was very worried about what was happening. I also asked him about school and wondered why he had been expelled. He said that this was because he had wrecked the class and caused trouble. I asked him why he did that. He said he just does it, he doesn't think at the time, he just goes ahead and does it. He could control himself if he really tried, if he stayed still for a while, but he would then be told off for not working—but really he was just trying to calm himself down. The work itself was not hard; he could read and was good at maths, although he was not good at doing stories.

I asked him what he would like to happen. he said to go to another school if possible, though he thought it unlikely that this would happen. He said something about having to go into care if he was going to get help, and he could not understand why he could not stay at home; he was very annoyed that this might have to happen. He gave me the impression of being a bright boy who thought and worried a great deal about himself. I thought he was in urgent need of seeing a child psychotherapist for intensive help. He himself said that he was not against seeing somebody.

He had few friends now, as it seemed he had alienated them by his behaviour. He gave the picture of an isolated boy with few social contact outside his immediate family. Like his brother he liked having contact with his mother, but was also concerned about her health. He described her as kind, but as having an illness she was born with. He was happy with his aunt who was kind, and he did not want the situation with her to change.

Overall, I had the picture of a boy who was very preoccupied with what was happening to him, and that he perhaps did not have the means at that time to be able to understand what was going on in his mind. He became easily angry and frustrated and also destructive, so much so that he had been permanently excluded from his local mainstream school. This was, in my view, a boy who urgently needed intensive therapeutic input, the details of which I outlined at the end of the report.

Interview with aunt

She said that Steven had been a problem since he was one year old, and that he had been excluded from nursery when he was four. He had had no treatment since then. Ritalin had been tried but with no effect, otherwise there had been no help offered. I agreed with her when she stressed the urgency of the situation. She agreed that he had a more positive side, in that he was very bright, which was even more of a tragedy. Steven was reading the newspapers before nursery school.

She came from a large and close family. She still saw her parents regularly. Her ill sister was the only one with major problems. They used to get on, but she now could not trust her because she had let the children down so often. I wondered what she herself felt about having someone else's children. She said that she loved children. She had never managed to become pregnant, and so she was happy to be the children's mother.

They were her life, though they could also be frustrating, particularly Steven. She had not worked since having them.

Overall, I found her a very caring and capable mother who had looked after the children for much of their lives. The children in turn loved her, and considered her their primary caretaker. She had been the steady figure in their lives and she was a strong and stable person. I also felt that she was absolutely right to be worried about Steven.

Interview with mother and children

The children's mother came late to the assessment, having apparently been given the wrong time. Despite this, I managed to see her with the children for a while, to get a feel of what they were like together, even though this was somewhat difficult as the children were tired and hungry by that time. Indeed, I had to call a halt to the meeting when Steven began to become increasingly aggressive. The aunt had been able to be more firm with him and Simon, but that was also early on in the assessment.

Mother showed affection towards the boys when she picked them up. In my room, mother mentioned that she had just seen them the day before for the afternoon, when they went to the park with a friend of hers. Generally she tried to take them to the shops or the park and then spend some time with both of them individually. She said that she tended to allow them to do what they wanted so that they could make a lot of noise and have discos. I did wonder at that point whether she was good at allowing them freedom, but not so good at being clear about giving boundaries and being firm.

I asked how contacts were at the moment, and she said fine. Steven had a few arguments, but generally they behaved. They understood that she was not well, and when she became quiet they realized she was not with it. Most of the time she coped with the situation fine. Sometimes she could feel herself getting anxious about them being bored and that she was not a proper mother. Steven seemed most worried about this, and she felt he needed one-to-one help. She was worried about him. At that point, Steven started to kick my toy box quite violently. I had to be strict with him and told him this was unacceptable, and for the first time I had a glimpse of what he could really be like.

Mother continued to say that the aunt was doing a good job and that she was very positive about her. After about fifteen minutes the children became increasingly difficult, fighting and shouting and competing for toys, and so I had to stop the meeting for fear of things getting completely out of hand. Mother kissed them good-bye and I took them down to the aunt, who then left with them.

Interview with mother

I asked the mother about the issue of contact. She said she was happy with the way things were for the moment. the children were happy and her sister was doing a very good job. So long as she and her sister could communicate things were OK. She realized that she herself was not fit to look after the children. She had no desire to increase the contact, especially now.

She mentioned that she had problems with drink, addiction to cannabis, panic attacks, and manic depression, all of which she was having help with. She was living with her parents at that moment, which had helped to stabilize her situation. When she was ill she found it difficult to see the children, but they understood that she can get ill and so could not see them. I asked about the friend she had taken to the contact the previous day. He was just a friend. She did not have a boyfriend at the moment, and I emphasized the need to make sure that she was more circumspect about men appearing without warning at contacts, particularly as she had had difficult relationships with them in the past, which had affected the children. I also tried to talk with her about the issue of providing firmer boundaries during contact, though she had difficulty grasping what I was saying.

Overall, the mother was someone with long-standing mental health problems of which she was aware and was currently trying to address. She was in a more stable state partly due to living with her parents. So long as the current arrangements were satisfactory, neither she nor anybody else saw the necessity for changing things. I also had the impression that it was helpful for the children to have some contact with her because of their anxieties about her. They were both worried about her illness, and so it seemed better for them to be reassured that she was stable rather than worry about her being ill, though there were also concerns that her lack of providing boundaries during contact might in itself make the boys anxious.

Documents

The reports provided mainly described in detail the mother's long psychiatric history, as well as the extensive disruptions in the early life of the boys due to their parents' chaotic lifestyle. A recent comprehensive psychiatric assessment of the mother's strengths and weaknesses noted that she had been well for several months, following a period of escalating substance misuse with associated depression. When unwell she required extensive support, medication, psychological treatment and, on occasions, hospitalization. The psychiatrist noted her dependent and emotionally unstable personality traits, and the fact that she had a tendency to act impulsively, particularly at times of stress. He was not able to advise the court on a firm prognosis. Essentially, it depended upon how much she was willing to limit her alcohol and cannabis consumption, as well as her ability to deal with her social situation.

The reports showed that there had been concerns about Steven's behaviour at school for some years. He was aggressive and also had severe temper tantrums, requiring the intervention of staff to stop him from injuring himself or others. The local clinic diagnosed that he was suffering from a severe adjustment disorder, but no therapeutic plan was put in place.

Conclusions

I commented that it seemed inappropriate to explain Steven's increasingly difficult behaviour as a result of disrupted contact with his mother, as the contact arrangement had been stable for several months. Clearly, his difficulties were long-standing and had become internalized. It was my view that he was in urgent need of a intensive treatment package, including psychotherapeutic help, ideally coupled with some sort of therapeutic environment. He did seem to respond to talking when I saw him, and the aunt was keen on him getting such help. While it was important to try and deal with disruptive children within their own schools, a boy such as this might need to attend an educational support unit, if there were one locally. Child psychotherapy might have to be bought in. Alternatively, he could attend a day centre for such vulnerable children where there would be a mixture of educational, therapeutic, and environmental help. The problem, as is so often the case, was that no such facilities were available locally. But unless such intervention were offered soon, one could foresee that he would deteriorate further. As a last resort, the local authority might have to consider sending him to a residential unit on his own.

I then addressed the six questions that I was given in the instructions.

In question one I was asked what, in my opinion, was the appropriate level of contact for the children to have with their mother. The answer to this was clearly that the current fortnightly arrangement was the appropriate level of contact. None of the parties now wanted to increase this, and this could only happen if the sisters came to a mutually agreeable arrangement.

Question two asked how contact arrangements bar the boys could best be addressed. I felt that the needs and requirements of the boys were best addressed by maintaining the current level of contact, with perhaps the occasional extra meeting. I was not convinced that any extra time with their mother would be beneficial.

The third question was concerned with the best way of arranging contact to prevent any inconsistencies between the benefit of contact to the boys and the dangers of contact being to their detriment. The best way of arranging contact was for the mother and aunt to be in effective communication with one another. So long as this could continue, then inconsistencies could be avoided. However, should the situation deteriorate again, the issue of contact would have to be reconsidered.

Question four asked for my opinion on what effect the introduction of new partners, or the reintroduction of the father, would have on the boys, their mental health and emotional well-being. I thought that at that point there should be no introduction of either the father (who was off the scene) or any partners. The reason for this was that the children had already been subjected to considerable disruption earlier in their lives, and that they now needed consistency and security. To this end, the current situation should be maintained as long as possible. In addition, one had to accept the fact that the mother had a long history of becoming involved with unsuitable partners. She might well feel that a new partner was going to be the answer to her problems, and might become convinced of this in the future, but any new partner would have to be rigorously assessed before being allowed to see the boys.

I was then asked, in question five, that if any such partner were to be introduced, how this should occur. Ultimately, the social services department needed to make the assessment of their suitability, and the aunt, who had the primary care of the children, would also have to be consulted.

The final question asked whether the level of mental health support to the family in general, and Steven in particular, was adequate, and, if not, how the level of provision could be improved. As I had already indicated, I felt strongly that the level of support offered to Steven was inadequate. He needed experienced and specialized help for his considerable emotional and behavioural difficulties. While there may have been a view that his difficulties were simply an expression of the uncertainty of contact arrangements, it was my view that he now had his own problems that urgently needed expert attention.

The eventual outcome of my assessment was that Steven did eventually have more appropriate help, but it took a long time to set up.

Further points

The various examples illustrate the often complex nature of situations where the expert is asked to give an opinion about issues of contact. Indeed, expert opinion is usually sought in those situations where there is conflict between one or more of the various parties: the carers, the birth family, the children, and the workers. It is even more important, then, for the expert not to be drawn into the conflict, but to retain their independence, as well as providing an opportunity for the various parties to reflect on what has been happening and what is best for the children. It is also important not to be too dogmatic about making recommendations regarding frequency of contact, unless the situation is very clear, such as when there is a very abusive partner.

Unfortunately, it can be difficult to facilitate change in what may have become quite rigid and oppositional positions, as shown in some of the examples described. Clearly, in order to provide a framework for thinking about contact issues, there needs to be a thorough assessment of the child's best interests. The examples in this chapter are limited to those situations where the independent expert is at work; in the next chapter, there will be clinical material involving multi-disciplinary working with a conflictual system around the family in rehabilitation issues, where contact with a birth parent may lead to an attempt to return the child to them or remove them permanently from their care. Given the strong feelings about removing children from their parents, let alone when trying to keep them with a disturbed parent, it is not surprising that such situations involve managing conflict, and can test to the limit workers' capacity to retain their ability to reflect on what is best for the child while trying to be fair to the parents.

Observations of contact between a parent and child over a period of time may be crucial to determining whether or not a parent should continue to have the same level of contact, should stop having contact, or should move to having more contact and possibly even resume full- or part-time care of their child. The expert, as has been described in some of the examples, can observe one or more contacts themselves, looking at what happens when the parents and children come together, what happens during the contact itself and how leave taking is managed. But it may also be important to have information about how contact has been managed over some months, and for that detailed and preferably skilled contact notes are essential.

In general, there is an assumption that contact will occur unless there are strong grounds for not having any. Grounds for not having contact are more obvious when the child is a baby and needs to have a primary attachment to their caretaker; less obvious when the child is older and already has a strong attachment to a parent, even if they are unable to provide a safe enough environment to look after them on a daily basis. The expert will need to include in their report clear arguments for or against contact, and whether or not any contact should be direct or indirect, based upon the criteria outlined by Sturge and Glaser (2000).

When contact is direct, then there will have to be decisions made about face to face and telephone contact, and with whom the contact should take place; that is, with the birth parents and any other members of the family and/or significant other people. There will need to be decisions about where it should happen, when, the frequency, the duration, who should be present, and the level of any supervision. Such "micro" decisions should be able to be made by the local social work department, once the overall opinion has been given; but occasionally the expert may be asked to facilitate or supervise the contact arrangements. Indirect contact can be via letters, presents, school reports, exchange of information, through a third party such as social services, or direct to the carers or adopters.

Finally, it is worth pointing out that the child's needs and wishes will change over time, and that whatever opinion is given about contact, it can only reflect opinion at that particular time. As mentioned before, contact arrangements cannot be fixed in stone forever, but have to be reasonably flexible and sustainable over time. Many adolescents wish to see their birth parent at some time, even if contact has been stopped, and despite what professionals may think about the wisdom of so doing. The adolescent may need considerable help in managing such renewed contact if it is not going to be disastrous to their current relationships.

They may well continue to retain fantasies about why they were removed from their parent, or have an idealized view of the absent parent, particularly if they have had no direct contact with them and hence no opportunity to test out the reality of the parent for themselves. As described by Baker (1995), in order for contact to be sustainable over the years after removal, the contact relatives need to support the new placement not just be compliant. The contact relative needs to accept the child's need to attach to the new carers; there needs to be harmony between the old and new carers, for the child's sake, and agreement about why the child is unable to remain with their birth parents, an agreement based on truth not fantasy, though the details may not need to be told all at once. However, it must be said that, however well the contacts are arranged, the child may well continue to feel responsible for their removal, or continue to retain unrealistic fantasies about their birth parents; and in those circumstances, they may well need specialized help in the form of some kind of psychotherapy in order to come to terms with their past.

To summarize arguments *for* contact:

- it seems to be protective against breakdown of the new placement
- it can be supportive of the new placement
- it recognizes that children, particularly late placed children, will later seek their birth parents and may even go back to them
- if the child's wishes are strongly in favour—it supports the child's sense of identity
- it can help reality testing of child/parent relationships—it can help to repair damaged relationships

To summarize arguments *against* contact:

- danger of repetition of abusing situation which led to the child's removal—danger of undermining new placement—risk of divided loyalty for the child
- not in child's interest if parent is severely ill, threatening, abusing drugs and/or alcohol—not in child's interest if parent is unreliable and constantly fails contact appointments—can keep alive unrealistic hopes about rehabilitation
- can perpetuate ambivalent relationship with a rejecting parent

CHAPTER FIVE

Rehabilitation issues: remove children or keep them with their parents?

General points

Deciding whether or not a child should be removed from their parents, or deciding that an attempt should be made to return them once they have been removed, can be one of the most difficult and complex decisions facing the professionals working with children and families. For this reason, assessment of such families should usually be undertaken within a multi-disciplinary team, where different views can contribute to the clinical picture and extensive discussion of issues can take place. A single jointly instructed expert can have a role in looking at a complex situation as an outsider. They may be able to look at the papers and give some guidelines about how to proceed and the potential prospects for rehabilitation. Or they may see the parents as a preliminary to a more extensive assessment, either to rule out the possibility of rehabilitation if the parents are, for example, devoid of insight, or, on the contrary, display a willingness and ability to be assessed fully. But it is difficult to give a final view about the prospects for rehabilitation without a comprehensive multi-disciplinary assessment.

The kinds of families for whom there is the issue of whether or not to proceed with rehabilitation are often disturbed, and also cause considerable disturbance in their professional network. Large amounts of anxiety, splitting between workers, and disputes about what should happen are common with the workers, and this may lead to reflex responses rather than measured action, or else paralysis and drift, with undue delay in making appropriate decisions. The examples from this chapter are taken from work with such disturbed families at the Cassel Hospital, a centre of excellence for the psychotherapeutic treatment of families, adolescents and adults.

The family service at the Cassel Hospital provides out-patient, day patient and residential facilities to assess and, where possible, treat multi-problem families from the whole country. The service has built up extensive experience of undertaking the arduous and sometimes nerve-racking task of rehabilitating families for which other forms of treatment have failed, been insufficient, or lacking. The Cassel approach is from an "applied" psychoanalytical viewpoint, which looks at unconscious factors in the individual and their family, but also takes account of the family's day-to-day behaviour and whole ways of relating, as will be illustrated in the examples in this chapter.

As I have already indicated elsewhere (Kennedy, 1997b), there are three essential questions that are raised time and again when making family assessments of problem families, where the issue of whether or not the child should remain with their parents is the main one.

- What is the ability of the parents in question to look after their child?
- Are the children safe with their parents?
- Should the family be given a chance to stay together, despite major problems, and when should rehabilitation be abandoned or not even attempted?

A thorough assessment of parenting capacities is the basis for providing answers about questions of children's safety and the chances of a successful rehabilitation outcome. Once the quality of the parents' relationship with their children is established, it is possible to have an idea of how safe the children are in their care. In addition, there will need to be a clinical judgement of how much responsibility the parents can take for how they have treated their children in the past, as indicated in the chapter on assessment. If parents deny past abuse, then it makes it virtually impossible to begin a rehabilitation programme. If a family can acknowledge that they have problems, that these problems are not just the fault of some external agency, that they are willing to accept help and are also willing to change, then one should seriously consider the possibility of rehabilitation.

Assessing capacity to change is the key to rehabilitation work, and for this reason it is particularly difficult and artificial to distinguish rigidly between assessment and treatment in these kinds of cases. As there are ongoing risks in working with these families, the therapeutic work involves constant monitoring and assessing of the parents' capacity to change and the sustainability of any changes over time.

Other issues relevant to decision-making around rehabilitation include the following:

The time scale of the child has to be taken into account, and whether or not this dovetails with the assessment of the parents' capacity for change. A delicate balance has to be drawn between giving the parents another chance and how this may affect the child's ability to make attachments at any given age (see Kennedy, 1997b.) Thus, a baby's needs are the most urgent, as adoptions have a greater chance of success when the adoptee is a baby capable of making early, long-lasting attachments. If the child has reached the age of eight or nine years, it is probable that there will be existing damage from a disordered attachment, and so there may not be undue harm if additional time were given to the assessment.

Because of the time scale issues, it is important to make assessments for rehabilitation as soon as possible. Undue delay in decision-making is unfortunately quite common, because of pressure of work on agencies, because of prolonged litigation in court, and because these are often complex situations requiring considerable amounts of staff time.

It can be tempting to side-step a thorough assessment and make a quick decision, such as removing a child, rather than face the complexity of the issues. It is also worth adding that it is difficult for the parents in these situations as well as for the children. The parent undergoing an assessment has to show what they are capable of; they have to prove that their parenting skills are adequate. At the same time they have to face the possibility of losing their child. One cannot underestimate the pain and conflict that this necessary situation may cause to the anxious parent. Of course, at least they may know that they are being given a chance with their child, and this may mitigate the parents' distress.

Overall, one is trying to strike a balance between the rehabilitation of children to their families and their permanent placement outside the birth family. It is worth mentioning at this point that such a balance is only an issue because of the particular overall system in which these decisions are made. A different social and legal system leads to different kinds of child protection practice. For example, this kind of judgement is rare in France. Children's judges there, for example, cannot make an order permanently separating a child from their birth parents, and although this power is available to a higher court it is very rarely used. Thus, adoption in these circumstances is rare in France. This situation reflects different cultural assumptions about the primacy of kinship and blood relations (see Cooper, Freund, Grevot, Hetherington, & Pitts, 1992). The limits of the judges' powers in France reflect and reinforce these assumptions. They also imply that social work and therapeutic effort in France is primarily directed towards rehabilitation and rarely towards removal along English lines. While it is impossible simply to transplant a way of working with families from one country to another without having the cultural and social backing of so doing, it may well be worth looking seriously at European practice.

Fostering and adoption

When coming to decisions about whether or not a family should be rehabilitated, the issue of whether adoption or long-term fostering would be a better option clearly has to be addressed, and certainly at the very least remains in the background. Placing a child in an adoptive or alternative permanent home will obviously have a major impact on their lives, and so one has to be as certain as one can be that this is the decision that is genuinely in the child's best interests, or, sometimes, in the child's least worst interests, that is, what is least detrimental to the child (see Goldstein, Freud, & Solnit, 1973). There may be very good reasons for removing a child from the birth parents, but at some point from adolescence onwards the child usually wants to see them, with varying results. For some children it can be helpful to make such contact, while with others, particularly where the adopters have never faced this possibility, this contact may provoke disturbance and even breakdown in family relations. Removal of children who can still remember their parents and who have strong, if ambivalent attachments, to them, will have a different impact from those who are too young to recall their early experiences. None the less, even the latter children often wish to make contact with their birth parents. Providing for some kind of ongoing direct or indirect contact for at least the older adopted child may minimize the risk of subsequent disruption, but may also interfere with the continuing stability of the adopted home.

When it comes to considering what happens later in life, there may be benefits of attempting rehabilitation, even if it is unsuccessful. The adolescent who looks over the past files may find that at least there had been an effort to rehabilitate the family, and this may help them with their own sense of identity; it may lessen the feeling that they were responsible for the past breakdown, or reduce the fantasy that they should have remained with their family of origin.

Adoption is usually recommended for a baby and younger children, as there are more realistic prospects of finding an adoptive family for them. The older the child the more difficult it is to find adopters, for obvious reasons—most people prefer to have children who will see them as their mother and father, and this is more likely with a young child with no memory of a birth parent. Also, the older the child the more likely it is to have significant problems, and most adoptive parents are put off by a problem child. There are, of course, adopters willing to take on older and more difficult children, but they are not easy to find, and the search for them can delay finding a permanent placement for many months. Delay is a main issue in dealing with permanency decisions. Because of the complexity of many of the situations where removing a child is being considered, there is a great risk of undue delay in making a final decision. While it is important, where possible, to give the birth parents a chance of continuing to look after their children, this has to be balanced against the present and potential risks to the child of so doing, and the inevitable delay that will be caused. It is of course vital to provide continuous and stable relationships for the child as soon as possible (see Goldstein, Freud. & Solnit, 1973). The longer one waits before providing such relationships, the worse the outcome may be for the child.

However, it can be just as damaging, in both the short and the long term, if a bad decision is made for the child's future, and it is necessary to beware of a temptation to by-pass all assessment and just remove a child and place them for adoption. While this may be appropriate in situations where a parent has shown no significant change in circumstances or capacity to care for a child, it is usually best practice to make sure there is a comprehensive and speedy assessment of the family before making a final decision about permanency. Unfortunately, the reality in the field is that services are stretched and there is often a great shortage of social workers—indeed, some social work departments currently have at least twenty-five per cent of their social work posts vacant. These kinds of assessments are time consuming and need the involvement of several staff, hence they are relatively costly. Sometimes specialized resources, such as the Cassel Hospital service can offer, are required in order to produce an adequate assessment, and there is often an in initial reluctance to find the appropriate funds for such place-ments. Thus, the courts often have to intervene to order an assess-ment, prolonging the delay even further as well as adding to the costs through the expensive litigation process.

Parallel planning is the best option while assessments are being undertaken. This can reduce the delays in the adoption process by having much of the bureaucratic decision-making sorted out, so that if rehabilitation is not feasible, the adoption can get under way. However, parallel planning is difficult for the birth parents to cope with. It certainly increases their anxiety and their sense of persecu-tion, which may interfere with their ability to cooperate with the assessment process, but this difficulty has to be weighed against the advantages of reducing delay in decision-making. Short-term foster carers have an important role in giving a child some stability while decisions are being made. They can also have a useful, if difficult, role in the rehabilitation process, as they can provide the stable home until a family can take on the permanent care of the child for themselves. Long-term fostering is often the placement of choice for the older child with a strong, if ambivalent, attachment to the birth parents, as it can provide for ongoing contact, and, even, at times, some kind of shared care arrangement.

The risk assessment

A common request made by referrers with the multi-problem family is not only to look at the prospects for rehabilitation, but also to look at the family with regard to the potential risks to the child. While there is an element of risk evaluation with all family assessments, these are usually situations of fairly high risk to a child; for example, when there have been serious, sometimes fatal, injuries to a previous child.

In order to help make clinical judgements of such cases, one may divide risks to a child into (a) general risks and (b) specific risks.

General risks

Assessment of risk to a child refers first of all to the degree to which a child may be subjected to significant harm as a result of emotional, physical, or sexual abuse. Thus, any assessment of risk needs to start with the basic assessment of the child's welfare, well-being, and safety within their family of origin or substitute family, or during contact with a parent or relative. This remains the basis or background for any assessment of specific risks. The assessment framework provides the foundation for this, and will include assessment of

1. the child's developmental needs;
2. family and environmental factors;
3. parenting capacity, as already discussed in the chapter on family assessments.

One of the main issues a risk assessment needs to address is the degree to which a child may be subjected to repeated violence; that is, the risk of a repetition of a severe injury, with the occasional risk of subsequent death. It is well recognized (see Bentovim, 1992) that violence within the family is more likely when there are abnormal patterns of attachment between parents and children, a disorder within one or more of the parents, where there is a dysfunctional parental relationship, and/or abnormal family interactions. Hence, the importance in the assessment of general risk to make detailed observations of attachment patterns, of the personality of each parent, of the parental relationship, and the whole family relationships and dynamics, including intergenerational issues.

Typical abnormal attachment patterns include insecure attachments—such as avoidant, ambivalent, or disorganized attachments (see Chapter Two).

Factors that predispose a parent to present risk to a child include severe mental illness and severe personality disorder, inability to take responsibility for actions, including past abuse, externalization of emotions, and inability to face emotions and to empathize with a child.

Risk factors in the parental relationship include ongoing violence between the couple, inability to communicate verbally, and inability to remain child focused.

Risk factors within the family system include blurring of boundaries between members, inability to differentiate child and adult members, externalization of emotions, excessive splitting and projection, and severe scapegoating.

Factors *reducing* general risk from the parent towards the child include taking responsibility for past abuse, ability to put the needs of the child first, recognition of the need for help, potential for change observed and sustained over time, cooperation with professionals, and positive response to therapeutic help.

Specific risk

These are to be seen in the context of the assessment of general risk, which provides the background to more specific issues, usually concerning the risks to a new child. These are often *high risk* situations. Typical issues include the following, with various combinations:

- Major safety issues such as recurrence of severe emotional, physical, or sexual abuse. Previous dead child under suspicious circumstances, but no clarification of cause of death.
- Previous dead child, neither parent the clear perpetrator, yet suspicions of both remain.
- Previous dead child, one parent being the obvious perpetrator, and the other parent failing to protect.
- Previous dead child and both parents perpetrators.
- Previous dead child, one parent responsible and the other, a new partner.

The main issues to be faced around these high risk situations are:

- to assess whether or not the circumstances around the new child are significantly different from those when the previous child was injured or killed;
- how the circumstances may be different;
- whether one or both parents in a relationship are a risk to the child

In order to assess the new situation one needs to look at

- the current safety of the child;
- the likelihood of repeated violence;
- the degree to which a perpetrator owns up to previous violence and abuse, which probably has a high degree of correlation with a reduction of future risk. It requires detailed attention to past events of abuse, but may take some time to elicit; it may require considerable skill in allowing the abusing parent to open up, when they may have dealt with their past behaviour by denial or repression. It can also be difficult to elicit when they fear losing their new child, or when they have to bond to a new baby;
- the degree of insight into past behaviour;
- the degree of repetition of past abusive behaviour and violent relationships.

Finally, and probably most difficult of all, it is necessary to give some indication of degree of risk to the child. This is usually seen in terns of low, medium or high risk. Such estimates can only be put forward after all the information from the assessment of general and specific risk is put together. Clearly, when it comes to considering rehabilitation of a family, one will want to see how the risk changes over time, moving from, for example, high to medium and then to low risk. Without such shifts rehabilitation is unlikely to be a feasible option.

Assessment of risk in contact issues is no different from the above, in that there needs to be an assessment of general risk as well as an assessment of the specific issues concerned with the nature and frequency of any contact. The main issues about risk at unsupervised contact concern the risk of emotional, physical, or sexual abuse. The main risk issue with supervised contact is that the contact might prejudice the new placement, and that this outweighs the various advantages of maintaining contact as summarized by Sturge and Glaser (2000) and discussed in the previous chapter.

Example one

Single father and baby

BACKGROUND

Mr A, in his thirties, was originally seen for an out-patient consultation with his teenage partner and their baby "Liam", aged three months. The mother had a very deprived upbringing. She had been severely neglected by her parents and was then adopted at about the age of six. She was subsequently sexually abused by a member of the adoptive family as she went into puberty, although she did not tell anyone. This was followed by years of disturbed behaviour. However, by the time of the interviews with both myself and the local authority's independent expert, she seemed to have matured. Mr A had an emotionally and socially deprived upbringing in a large and poor family. There was considerable conflict between his parents, and he and his siblings were often physically punished. His father was a drinker and a gambler, and Mr A was sent by his mother to try to stop him from losing money. Mr A married early in order to escape his family, and had children, but the marriage did not last. By the time of the interview, he had cut himself off from his ex-wife and children, and rarely had any contact with his family of origin.

With regard to their relationship, both described that the difference in their ages had been a difficulty at the start. They were first of all friends, but this gradually developed into a relationship. She felt relaxed with him and grew to trust him—the first man she felt able to trust. She also explained that she now spoke a lot more for herself and felt more confident. Mr A talked about getting to know the mother as someone with problems, who was not getting proper support from social services, with whom he was still very angry. He, on the other hand, had provided her with security.

After Liam's birth, the mother was placed in a foster home with him, with Mr A having some contact. However, she eventually walked out of the placement, supposedly because there was too much competition from the foster mother. Liam was placed with a new foster parent with a view to permanency being sorted out. Mr A and his partner wished to have him in their care. There had never been a period in which they were allowed to have him in their combined care.

I felt that it was reasonable to go ahead with an intensive residential assessment of the couple and the baby, and this was supported by the other expert, though the couple would need to come on their own for a while, in order to test out their stability before proceeding with an admission of the baby. With this in mind, a nursing home assessment took place at the couple's flat, which in fact revealed worrying features of the situation. The father was very defended against revealing any vulnerability and reluctant to consider what he got out of the relationship with his much younger and needy partner The couple denied having any child-care problems, though when the baby was brought by the social worker the mother had difficulties responding appropriately to the baby's cues. However, she did respond reasonably to suggestions from the nurses, while on the other hand the father was reluctant to admit that he might be wrong or need some guidance. The couple were also rather boundary-less. During the visit, two young women walked into the flat for a chat, through the open door, and it was only after the nurses were fairly assertive about the importance of the meeting, that the visitors were asked by the couple to leave and the door was finally shut.

In fact, shortly after this visit, the couple's relationship deteriorated, there was some kind of row and then they split up; there seemed no possibility of working with either of them separately. The expert view was that the baby should go for adoption.

It was thus a great surprise when, several months later, I was contacted again by Mr A's solicitors for a view about what should happen to Liam. The situation had been allowed to drift. He was still in foster care, there were no clear plans about his future, the mother was out of the picture as a potential carer as she had been disturbed again, but the father had maintained regular contact with his son. The contact visits generally went well; there were no major concerns about his handling of the baby, but the local authority were against him being considered as a potential carer because of his antagonistic attitude towards them and because of his rather unsettled lifestyle. He continued to live in run-down accommodation and insisted on retaining contact with Liam's mother, though he also insisted that they were no longer in a relationship. He explained that he was concerned about her, as she was receiving no support from the professionals.

I saw him again, on his own, and was struck by his commitment over several months to his son. Although he continued to maintain an oppositional attitude to social services, he was willing to consider an assessment at the Cassel, if that would help him get his child back. I had always found him reasonably engageable, perhaps because he found me a less threatening authority figure, who was trying to give him a chance.

Residential assessment

It took some time to set up a full assessment with him and his son, involving two court appearances, a teleconference with the other expert, and much correspondence between the solicitors, the local authority, and myself, clarifying a number of issues concerned with the risks of an assessment. One main issue that came up repeatedly concerned the nature of the attachment between Liam and his father. There were assertions that this attachment was poor, despite evidence to the contrary, including the observations of one of our own child psychotherapists. The issue then concerned the risk of moving him away from the foster carer, to whom he was well attached, to the father's care, and the fear that this might cause irre-versible damage. However, the fact was that if Liam was going for adoption, he would have to lose the attachment to his foster carer anyway. I made the point that if rehabilitation worked, then Liam would not have to lose the attachment to his father, nor have to make a new attachment to adopters, and that this possibility had not been considered.

There was considerable opposition from social services to the possibility of the father having a chance with his son, while the Children's Guardian stayed somewhat on the fence. Initially, Mr A was only allowed to come to the hospital on his own for a couple of weeks, in order to test out his motivation for help, and to see whether or not he would cooperate with any further assessment. He managed this admission surprisingly well. He cooperated with the programme, attended therapeutic structures and was generally quite helpful around the unit. His fierce independence and anti-authority stance remained, but were easily manageable. We kept him at the hospital until the next hearing, even though he was unfunded, and eventually, following my appearance in court, an order was made under section 38(6) of the Children Act directing the local authority to pay for an assessment of father and son, some four months after I had again become involved with assessing Mr A. One could argue of course that the time and considerable amounts of money spent on litigation in this case could have been better spent getting on with the assessment in the first place.

Outcome of assessment

The outcome of the assessment was our recommending that Liam be rehabilitated to his father's care, preferably though a programme at the Cassel. The assessment showed that Mr A had good parenting capacities. The main area of concern remained how much he was willing to work with professionals. However, it was the team's strong view that, despite his difficulties, Mr A had shown a general shift in his attitude and was more amenable to advice and support, and for that reason rehabilitation would be in the child's best interests.

In his therapy sessions, he often spoke about the social services' and Cassel's "systems", and their failings as helpful organizations. He would give examples of how he and others had been repeatedly let down by them. This constant talk seemed to be a defence against his anxiety over losing custody of his son, and also served as a defence against speaking about any anxieties he might have or worries he might have as a patient.

During his son's first week with him, Mr A was taken up with trying to settle him into a routine, and he was obviously torn by the various demands made on him. He found it difficult early on to cope with the pressures, and needed considerable help, but he began to speak more about his own childhood, and made some shift away from his position of an observer rather than a participant. As a child he seemed to have had frightening experiences of being left alone at hospital. Recalling these experiences helped him to become more in touch with what it was like for his son to be at the Cassel and having to leave his father for the foster home most weekends. Indeed, he was himself keenly aware of his own father's comings and goings. The picture of his mother remained shadowy—she exerted control over his weaker father—and he did not seem to have much of a sense of a parent figure who could take responsibility for a child and sort out worries. He had become adept at parenting himself, and had developed his own views about life as an alternative to the "system". Therapy sessions at times made him feel vulnerable and humiliated, yet at the same time he did open up occasionally, which seemed to indicate that he could make use of therapy.

The child psychotherapist, who saw him and Liam together, had a picture of a father and son who were developing a warm and trusting attachment. Liam struck the therapist at first as being placid and cheerful. She was surprised at how relatively uncurious and unfazed he seemed at being in a strange environment. In their first session together, Liam played contentedly with the toys his father gave him, only becoming fractious towards the end of their time.

By the end of the period of assessment, there was a marked shift in the father, who was able to acknowledge how stressful being at the Cassel must have been for Liam. He volunteered examples of behaviour Liam was displaying that showed his anxiety, and he seemed quite interested in thinking about this with the therapist. The father's softer tone and attitude enabled Liam to be much more explorative and curious. He seemed confident that father was there to help him if he got into difficulties. For example, when he got his foot trapped, he immediately turned to his father who was able to respond swiftly and appropriately.

The therapist had a picture of a father and son who were developing a warm, trusting attachment, in which the father was able to be a concerned and reliable father figure, and she recommended rehabilitation work for them both.

The family's nurse described how at first Mr A had difficulty in anticipating his son's reactions. For example, when Liam was on the swing in the hospital's playground, Mr A walked away, telling a another patient that he was going to get a cup of coffee but not telling Liam. Liam turned as far back as he could on the swing, and when he could no longer see his father, fear appeared on his face, only to be stopped by the patient soothing and reassuring him that his father would be back. A little later, Mr A gave Liam a cup while he was still on the swing. Liam wanted to drink but could not as the swing was still going. The other patient stopped the swing so he could drink.

Mr A was initially rather slow in feeding his son, and on one occasion it was noticed that Liam was still hungry when Mr A decided that Liam had had enough. Staff had to intervene so that Liam had more food.

However, the situation began to improve. Father showed more warmth towards Liam, and began to respond more effectively to Liam's needs. Liam began turning to his father more and more, and was able to play on his own when appropriate. At social services' request, night workers were booked to observe the family. Their reports were positive, describing adequate boundary setting, emotional warmth, good basic care, appropriate stimulation, and consistency. In the nursery, Liam became more clingy when father left him, yet also made good use of the nursery facilities. He was also beginning to verbalize more. Mr A made relationships in the hospital community. He was supportive of other patients and less of a loner.

Overall, it was clear how much change there had been, in that father was much more able to look after his son in a more consistent and emotionally available way. When they were first admitted, the father needed a considerable amount of help in order to attend to his son appropriately. However, as a result of this help, he soon became much more able to deal with the day-to-day aspects of parenting. We did hear that Liam showed some disturbance on returning to the foster home, but recovered quite quickly. He showed a similar pattern on going back to the hospital. It seemed most probable that at these times he was showing signs of confusion and disruption, and that this would decrease once his future was settled. The behaviour could not be explained by the father being a bad parent.

The main concern remained the father's own personality difficulties. While he did not have a formal personality disorder, he had a somewhat deprived upbringing and had found a way of coping with this by being self-sufficient and by creating his own rather rigid view of the world and the "system". Individual psychotherapy continued to show this problem, but there were also signs that he was able from time to time to listen more and allow his defences to drop. While expressing a wish to remain at the hospital for rehabilitation, he was also guarded, not surprisingly, about how much he could reveal of his dependency needs, given the lack of support from social services for his continuing to stay with his son.

Another other issue of concern was whether or not Mr A could deal with day-to-day affairs. This was a main task of the nursing work, and the nurse indicated that progress had been made in this area. There was also concern about whether or not Mr A was continuing to have a relationship with Liam's vulnerable mother, although he denied it.

At the assessment meeting, there was a unanimous view from the Cassel staff that Mr A and Liam should be rehabilitated. If this were to take place, it would occur in a number of graded stages. The first stage would involve preparing the home for Liam's return, with work both on the practicalities as well as the emotional impact on both of them of changing the situation. The next stage would involve gradually introducing Liam to the new home, leading up to the first overnight stay, and then after about three months, the first weekend stay. Around that time, the foster placement would end. There would then be a few months of consolidation work, involving preparing the family for their new life in their community.

The local authority continued to oppose rehabilitation. They also wanted to remove Liam until the final hearing, some two weeks after the assessment meeting. However, we argued that they should remain until a decision was to be reached.

In fact, the final hearing was to take place in the summer, when I was on annual leave. At court, the judge decided, because of the complexity of the case to postpone making a decision until my return. One had the impression that the judge was in favour of rehabilitation and was reluctant to remove Liam from his father, but had to contend with the law at that time, which did not enable him to order treatment. Unfortunately, there was no additional funding for this period, and Liam was returned to his foster carer, with the father having frequent access.

We tried to keep in touch with Mr A, but it was difficult for him to attend the hospital regularly, given the distances involved and his need to maintain contact with his son. This was an excruciatingly painful and uncertain period for Mr A and to some extent his son.

Just before the resumed final hearing was to take place we arranged for close observation of contact between Liam and Mr A and also between Liam and his foster carer, in order to be clear about the quality of Liam's attachments. In fact, he seemed well attached to both his carers, and was, perhaps surprisingly given the uncertainty of the situation, quite contented. The outcome was reasonably satisfactory in that, just at the last moment and the day before I was to appear in court, social services conceded that rehabilitation of father and son was the best option and put in place a detailed community rehabilitation plan, buying in twice weekly private psychotherapy as part of the package.

Example two

Two parents and then one

BACKGROUND

The B family consisted of mother, father, and two children, a boy aged five and a girl aged three. At the time of the referral by the parent's solicitor, the children were being fostered by their maternal grandparents. Concerns about the family centred on living conditions in the family home, which were squalid. There were also safety issues in the home. For example, there was no lighting in certain parts of the house, and the bathroom was being lit by a car battery attached to a torch. The children were neglected, both physically and emotionally, and showed increasing disturbance at school and elsewhere, as well as developmental delays. There were considerable concerns about the quality of the attachment and the levels of stimulation between the parents and the children. Community-based treatment over some time produced no change. The Guardian's solicitor obtained a report from a well known independent expert who recommended that the most likely setting where appropriate help could be given to this family was the Cassel Hospital.

Initial interview

In my initial interview with the family, I confirmed what other workers had found. The children were difficult to manage and there was a chaotic feeling for much of the session, with the parents unable to intervene effectively with their children. When I collected them from the waiting room the children rushed up the stairs, followed anxiously by myself, with the parents following behind me very slowly. The boy, "Mark", was difficult to relate to, as he rushed from one thing to another, my toys, objects in the room, the window, my video equipment (which was not being used). The girl, "Sophie", spent some time looking through the toys, but looked sad, rarely smiling. She did not speak in my presence—though she apparently did have some words, she did not like speaking in front of strangers.

When I asked the parents about their current situation, and mentioned the foster home and their contact arrangements, Mark took one of my folding chairs in order to sit at the table with the toys, rather than the chair next to the table. Throughout the interview, he would fold and unfold this chair from time to time, adding to the general chaos. When he started to draw his sister also wanted to draw. She tried to make some space on the table, but Mark would not let her, so she started moaning. Eventually the father intervened to help her, but mother remained frozen. When, later in the session, both children were playing chaotically with the folding chairs, pushing them around and folding and unfolding them, father said,

"Look what's happening. Social services say they never play together but they are." I pointed out that they were rather chaotic, and he replied that normally they just head for different parts of the room.

When I asked the parents why they were in their current situation, father tended to maintain an attitude that social services had gone beyond what they should have, and that they were always nitpicking. Things were bad in the past, but he maintained that they had improved, and just when they did the children were removed. He agreed that they had problems, but he maintained they were sorted out. The mother was less sure about this. When we went into the concerns about the state of their house, she explained that part of the problem was that she was depressed; but now that she was on antidepressants, she felt a lot better. They did agree, however, that they still had problems about hygiene and day-to-day care, even if father tended to say that things were better now.

I did try to obtain some detail about the children, but it was not really possible to take any coherent history with the children present; the interview was more about trying to stem the chaos, while observing the family relationships. The parents did tell me about the children's problems at school and of Mark's diagnosis of attention deficit disorder, for which Ritalin had been tried without success. They tried to explain the children's problems as the effect of allergies, by which time I had to be pretty firm about the parents' need to look at themselves and how they might be more in touch with their children's emotional needs.

Towards the end of the interview, I did press the parents on what help they would need. At that point the father admitted he had problems. He said he was not affectionate and wanted help with this. His wife had complained about it; she was a person who needed cuddles. He realized that he had not seen this in the past, and he was beginning to realize that he needed to change. I thought that at last there was a chink in his defensive armour. I certainly thought that aspects of the couple's relationship, in particular whether or not they could communicate and show affection to one another, must obviously been having a profound effect on the children, who appeared to feel out of touch with their parents.

Both parents were very keen on coming to the Cassel for help, and they saw it as a last resort to get their children back.

The family's social worker, who had accompanied them, explained that social services had tried everything possible without anything changing. The family, particularly the father, was resistant to change. From the local assessments, they felt that there was not enough change to warrant trying to rehabilitate the children. The problem was that they changed a little when support was put in, but then once support was removed the situation reverted again. The father was the most emotionally removed from the children, showing little emotional reaction.

My own view, supported by the independent expert and the Guardian, was that the family had not been given skilled enough intensive input. While I agreed that the situation was serious, with the real possibility that the children would have to be found a home away from the family, it was worthwhile trying a more intensive residential assessment before writing off the parents. I thought it most unlikely that ordinary outpatient intervention would help such a difficult family, because of their chaotic lifestyle and the children's substantial difficulties. There would be no harm in delaying a final decision, because these difficulties would need to be assessed in detail before any decision about permanency, and because of the age of the children. These were not very young children with few problems who could be easily placed; they were older and quite disturbed in their own right, and they could also have a thorough assessment of their emotional and educational needs.

Court of Appeal

Unusually, the Court of Appeal soon became involved in the decision about a Cassel assessment. This was because the local judge refused to make a section 38(6) order, which would have compelled the local authority to fund a Cassel assessment. The local authority maintained that they wished the family to be seen locally, despite the fact that they had tried for years to intervene with the family with little success. However, the independent expert maintained that any alternative to the Cassel would not be an equivalent service that could address the family's needs, and thus would not assist the court in making the assessment that was required through a residential placement.

Arguments were also raised by the local authority about the high cost of the Cassel, although their arguments, and their evidence, were not very well put together. Also, it then became clear that if the Cassel were not to be used, the family would not in fact receive any kind of residential input, even at a cheaper and less intensive resource then available (and subsequently closed).

While the original judge was favourably disposed to order the Cassel treatment, he interpreted the judgement of Mr Justice Holman in *Re M* to the effect that the prospects of success should be markedly better than even before a referral to the Cassel should be made, particularly in the light of the high costs involved. As the Guardian had put the prospects in this case as no better than even, then the judge decided "with a heavy heart" that he could not order a Cassel assessment. In fact, Mr Justice Holman found that the chances had to be around 50/50 for an initial assessment to take place; they did not have to be much better than that. I myself was in the witness box for nearly a whole day while Mr Justice Holman presided over the issue of whether or not a particular family should have a Cassel assessment.

The judge gave leave to appeal, and the issue of funding as well as the grounds for having a Cassel assessment were considered in detail at the Court of Appeal by Lord Justice Matthew Thorpe and Dame Elizabeth Butler-Sloss, President of the Family Division.

Lord Justice Thorpe, in his judgement, balanced the issue of funding with that of the benefit to the child and the local authority's responsibilities to children in general. While the court had to take into account potential difficulties over funding, it had to give proper weight to these other factors. He described the Cassel Hospital as:

> ... the resource of ultimate expertise and experience in this field, particularly for the residential psychotherapeutic assessment and treatment of parents and children as a whole family unit. Their expertise in assessing whether or not a family is treatable is unrivalled. [*Re B*, p. 709A]

He pointed out that the purpose of a residential may often be, as it was in this case, to assess the parents' capacity to respond to treatment intended to resolve or diminish emotional or psychological disorders currently disabling the parent from achieving an adequate standard of parenting. During that period of assessment psychotherapy may be offered, partly to assess the parents' capacity to enter into a therapeutic relationship, but at the same time initiating the necessary process of change. The primary purpose is to assess a present capacity, the capacity to accept treatment. One could add that from this follows that assessment and treatment often go hand in hand in these cases, and that what one is assessing is the capacity to change. However, such a capacity has to be observed over some time, in order to assess the sustainability of any change.

In fact, with the B family, the local authority produced such poor evidence for their funding difficulties, as well as poor alternative therapeutic resources for the family, that the appeal judges had no hesitation in ordering the Cassel assessment to take place. Dame Elizabeth also stated that while the specialist and expensive help offered by the Cassel was not needed in the majority of difficult cases, the Cassel had something enormously valuable to give to really difficult families such as the one under consideration for the benefit of the children, who are the concern of the local authority and the concern of the courts.

Outcome of assessment

The parents' difficulties both between themselves and with their children soon became very apparent. Mother revealed increasing disturbance in her own right, while the father often appeared cut off from what was happening. But it was the mother's often vulnerable state of mind that became of increasing concern.

The family settled into the hospital routine surprisingly well. Both parents accepted the "rules" and expectations of hospital life, and indeed were outwardly very compliant. However, they soon came across as very anxious and unsure about themselves, as individuals, as a couple, and as parents. Most of the nursing attention was focused around the mother, who needed a very firm and boundaried approach, as she had great difficulty in managing her feelings. She would often revert to a dependent and child-like position in her relationships.

In mother's individual therapy; her female therapist was struck by how much her general demeanour seemed to place her among the children as opposed to identifying her as a parent, an adult. This impression was subsequently reinforced as time went on. She described herself as "Daddy's girl", saying that "Dad is the best", he was "Dad number one". Her husband's father was "Dad number two", and her husband was "Dad number three". On the other hand, mothers were difficult for her. She could be very angry with her own mother, and hated her grandmother and mother-in-law. She consciously associated her dislike of housework with her dislike of these women. She did not want to be like them, so she did not do what they did—that is, to be a housewife who could keep a home tidy and in order. It was not surprising, then, that she struggled with the demands of motherhood and of being a responsible parent.

Mrs B agreed with this kind of understanding, but the problem was that she agreed with the therapist about virtually everything, as she was so desperate to please her, despite being a woman. Indeed, the transference seemed more paternal than maternal. Her refusal to do housework seemed related to a wish to keep her place as father's preferred daughter.

In his therapy, Mr B revealed a courteous, helpful manner, although he found it difficult to be very forthcoming. He found sessions difficult as he said that he did not like to speak unless he was sure he was correct. He preferred to listen to others. He believed he developed this trait as a result of being teased as a child for being overweight.

Although not forthcoming about his feelings, he was able to give details about facts and procedures in regard to his work, where he acted independently from any team.

Most of these sessions were dominated by his despair at his wife embarrassing him by her sometimes ill-considered and inappropriate remarks. Although he acknowledged that she could be loving towards the children, he felt hopeless about her inability to deal with everyday home life.

Despite his calm and friendly manner, the therapist picked up how angry he was, but how difficult it was for him to express his anger, which he had to keep under tight control.

In fact in the hospital, the father took on most of the practical care of the children. He was appropriately focused on them and kept them safe. The mother, however, appeared increasingly distracted and preoccupied. She paid more attention to her daughter Sophie than her son Mark, though only fleetingly.

Before the child psychotherapist saw Mark she interviewed the parents together. They both described him as a child who was quite difficult to understand and they struggled with him. The mother felt she never had a bond with him and that she always found it difficult relating to him, partly due to post natal depression. She also described how he looked after her when she was depressed.

Mark became increasingly upset and angry at this time, and also began occasional soiling. When the child psychotherapist first saw him, he presented as a child who was rather shy and apparently detached. She found it difficult to engage with him; he would not talk to her and would keep himself busy with plasticine or paper and crayons. In the first session he drew a snowman, evidence perhaps about the coldness he experienced in the sessions at first. Slowly, his play expanded and he started to use bricks. But when the therapist asked him questions about what he was doing, he would keep changing his explanations, as if he could not sustain his thoughts and plans. He was also concerned about things sticking together, and seemed increasingly desperate to please the therapist.

The therapist saw him initially as a child who was quite restricted in his ability to express his feelings and in his ability to relate. Often this came across as his being rather odd or difficult to understand. Then just before one of the last sessions before the assessment meeting, the mother told the therapist that Mark had witnessed her having a panic attack.

That day Mark found it hard to leave his mother and he regressed to being something of a baby. He clung to his mother and did not want to look at the therapist. In the end, he did not want to go to the session and the therapist accepted this but made it clear that he needed to be helped to come to the next one, which he did. He was then quite different, in that he was more able to use a wider range of toys in the room, particularly the baby toys. He kept asking the therapist questions about who she saw at the hospital and what she did with other children. He showed how creative he could be by suggesting various games to play and things to do. However, each time the therapist tried to explore things with him just by asking questions about what he was doing or by trying to understand what he had planned to do, he would stop that particular play and introduce something different. This revealed a sense of Mark's confusion or lack of consistency in his thinking.

He became particularly anxious towards the end of sessions, needing to go to the toilet, as if he could not bear some of the feelings that had been aroused. Just before the last session before the assessment meeting, mother warned the therapist that if she smelled something unpleasant it was to do with the fact that she had not had time to wash Mark. By this she meant that he had soiled himself. When the therapist tried to explore this with him, he made it clear that he did not want to talk about it and that it felt "uncomfortable". The therapist was left puzzled by what the mother had done, and wondered whether the mother might enact in a concrete and destructive way some of her feelings about her child going for therapy.

Overall, the therapist was concerned about Mark's emotional development, especially about his sense of self. He was a child with potential who responded well to a one-to-one situation where he could be listened to attentively. He needed that kind of experience in order to develop a more consistent self. He also seemed very deprived of real nurturing, and the therapist was concerned about what Mark carried on behalf of his parents. He appeared to show a more infantile or less developed side of himself in order to respond to his mother's needs and, perhaps, his father's absence.

In the hospital school Mark showed literacy and numeracy skills around National Curriculum level two, but was erratic in his capacity to apply himself to new learning. He often seemed to hold himself back, reluctant to wrestle with new ideas or ways of approaching his learning. He said several times that he wished he could be a baby, which seemed to equate with being cared for and protected from his own frustrations. He responded well to having stories read to him, but his behaviour could be testing of boundaries. He was verbally abusive to the teacher and spat at her as the assessment meeting came close, although he responded positively to clear rules about what was acceptable behaviour. Although he had accrued a diagnosis of attention deficit disorder from his local services, he did not show the kind of driven behaviour most evident in that condition. He responded to appropriate understanding and attention, and showed some willingness and ability to use educational input.

Sophie came across in her child therapy meetings as a sturdy three-year-old who engaged one with her open friendly gaze, but was unable to talk. She was seen with either or both parents in the room. She used gestures and vague noises to indicate what she wanted, and was very good at getting others to give her what she needed. It was observed how much her mother would intervene to help her and not encourage her to articulate what she wanted, as if she wanted Sophie to remain a baby.

Sophie tended to concentrate intensely but briefly on an activity before going on to the next thing. She would get a parent to help her undo the lids of toys, or take out some play dough, by pulling their arm and gesturing but not speaking. She revealed through her play anxiety about her body and potty training, which was delayed. She seemed to respond positively to the sessions and the chance to begin to have some of her conflicts articulated.

There was a contrast in Sophie's relationship with each parent. Mother described her as her "very special child", with whom she over-identified, and, as mentioned before, babied.

The father was able to talk more clearly about Sophie's emotional needs, but also tended to keep his distance from her. Rather than encourage her to speak, he would just respond to her gestures.

In the family meetings, there was some positive change. In the first meeting, there was a lot of fighting between the children, while both parents sat back unsure about how to intervene. Mother tried to keep Sophie on her lap and seemed unable to move from this stance. But in the second session, father began playing with the children, both of whom were more cooperative. The parents were able to talk about how easy it was for the mother to take over the conversation, while it was clear how much the children appreciated it when father was given a space to voice his feelings and thoughts.

At the assessment meeting, the parents expressed the view that the situation had been improving with the children. Sophie was beginning to make an effort to speak, and Mark was improved at the foster home. The couple were trying to be more consistent with the children. However, it was clear from the reports that there were considerable and long-standing difficulties in the family and a great deal of work for them to do before rehabilitation could be considered. The processing of emotions in the family seemed difficult for all family members. The father's emotional distance and the mother's difficulty in keeping an appropriate distance created a difficult environment for the children.

It was decided that a two-month period of work should take place in which the situation would be clarified. The aims of the work were for the parents to be more open and communicative; that the mother be encouraged to differentiate her needs from those of the children; and that issues about control and anger that the children displayed for the family as a whole be looked at in regular family sessions. We were to make a referral for Sophie for speech therapy, and there was also to be work with the grandparents around weekends and contacts.

Subsequent to the assessment

We tried to work with the mother and father together with the children, but soon came to realize that as much as the mother tried, it was just not in the children's interests to have her deal with them on a daily basis. She had become increasingly disruptive and unable to contain herself. She tended to spill out her thoughts inappropriately to the children and was unable to deal with boundaries. She would spill out all kinds of muddled thoughts and feelings about herself and the children, while her husband would not intervene. She continued to be unable to look after the children in an ordinary way, although he was able to do so, given nursing and patient support. Mark became increasingly angry and hostile, as well as preoccupied about safety. Sophie, who was seen on her own for her therapy, had begun to make progress, but then seemed to become stuck again.

It rapidly became clear that it was not possible to work with the couple towards their having the children. This left deciding between removal from both parents, or one parent having the children on their own. Clearly the mother was incapable of providing a consistent and emotionally safe environment for the children, and so we were left with the possibility of the father being the sole caretaker, a view strongly supported by the Children's Guardian. The father wished for this. By that time, he had come to the end of his tether with his wife. However, he was also still, not surprisingly, caught up in their relationship. It took a considerable amount of work to help the family deal with the mother's separation. But it was soon very clear that the children were much more settled without their mother.

Mr B managed the everyday care of the children well. He began to demonstrate more ability to think ahead and participate in things with regard to them. He began to have a new confidence and more of a voice in groups and meetings, and was using these areas to explore parenting issues. He was able to make sure the children's hygiene and personal care were attended to, and was able to take them out to play areas and places of interest at the weekend and evenings, where appropriate. He coped well with the pressures and demands on himself without resorting to frustration and anger. He still had feelings towards his wife, but they were manageable, even though she put pressure on him, through telephone contact and at her contact with the children, to have her back. In his therapy, he talked about coping with his wife's absence well, but worried about the future. He acknowledged that it was a relief not to have a third child to look after, and that he had been smothered by her and unable to think for himself. He just let her intrude everywhere. It was the same with his mother; it was as if he merged with both of them and was unable to feel separate. He was, however, more able to think about the children's needs as individuals, though he needed more help to understand his daughter.

Sophie's therapist noticed quite a shift in the sessions. She was beginning to use play to express some of her concerns and it was clear that she had a curiosity and a wish to develop that was not apparent when her mother was in the hospital. However, she also showed a preoccupation with babies and baby needs and a wish to have everything for herself. She showed how deprived a child she was, having lacked the maternal care and consistency that she needed. The father was more capable with her, but also found it difficult to recognize her unmet emotional needs. He saw the world in a concrete, factual way and it was hard for him to appreciate the anger and distress that Sophie probably felt and that would come out in due course. The speech therapy assessment revealed so little speech that this suggested that there was a mixed picture of possible neurological difficulties, developmental delay, and emotional problems.

Mark was much more settled around the hospital and pleased to have his father's attention. In his therapy sessions, he spent a lot of time using sellotape to try to stop access to his various toys. Eventually he removed the tape and began to display a number of sexual preoccupations. While such preoccupation was age appropriate, there was also a suspicion that he was trying to communicate anxieties about his relationship with his mother and how sexually intrusive she could be. There was no clear evidence suggesting actual abuse. In the school setting, he continued to show a wish to learn, but also great muddle and confusion in both his literacy and numeracy skills, and clearly needed continuing specialized help.

Overall, it was clear that this family had only recently begun to have some stability and consistency from their father. The children were progressing well, but the situation was fragile, and I recommended several months' further work to secure a safe rehabilitation to their home. The father also had to work through the separation from his wife and set up home as a single parent, which would take some time. Both children had considerable need of therapeutic input, and it would seem to wrong for them to break off treatment at this crucial point. We did, however, agree to some curtailing of our full programme, if the local services could take over the latter aspects of the rehabilitation.

Back to High Court

Unfortunately, social services opposed our plan. They thought the family should be discharged immediately and picked up by local services, with whom we had, in fact, been in contact. The social worker now believed that the situation was easy enough to deal with in the community, and, indeed, maintained that this was also the case. She and her manager maintained a rather strange attitude, in my view, which persisted months later at a follow-up workers' meeting—that this family was always easily treatable and that it had been a waste of time coming to the Cassel. They had to be reminded by both the Guardian and the independent expert of the severity of the problems, of the lack of progress made by local services, and by the fact that no one had ever though the father capable of taking on the family on his own. They remained unconvinced.

When it came to the High Court for a decision about further treatment, there was the usual huddle in the corridors. The usual question at that time about whether assessment or treatment was being proposed came up, rather than what was in the children's best interest. It was very helpful having the distinguished independent expert on board, and the combined effort of the both of us managed to persuade the local authority to agree to a three-month extension of the family's admission, during which there would be a gradual handover to the local services, including a family centre.

Subsequent progress

In fact, the family managed the rapid rehabilitation programme remarkably well. Mark was more settled. One of the main themes in his therapy was a wish to find a home, the sessions being a place where he felt he had found a home. He often set up situations where he looked after the therapist or where the therapist looked after him. This brought up the whole issue of him missing his mother, or missing a mother who could look after him. The therapy dealt with the difficult issue of why he had lost his mother, his feeling responsible for her and his fear that he had damaged her. In general he became more creative in the sessions, more able to have his own thoughts and to communicate his feelings. In the last session, he made a whale out of plasticine and then told the therapist that the whale had a problem with his heart. When they talked about Mark's problem with his heart about saying good-bye to the Cassel, he was very open and said that he did not want to leave the hospital. He obviously had strong and meaningful relationships there and he was quite worried about what would happen when he finally returned home.

Using the whale, he was able to talk about his fears that he would die for lack of nurturing, that he was not getting enough emotional nourishment, and of losing what he did get when he left the Cassel. He was also able to acknowledge his sadness about leaving, which was a significant change from before.

Sophie displayed real changes in her therapy. Her father's presence in the sessions was supportive; she was able to leave him to involve herself in her play, while turning to him for comfort if she were anxious. She was able to return to using symbolic play and used toys appropriately to communicate her concerns. The main themes of her play were around her need for mothering and her concerns about returning home.

Previously her therapist was worried about how often Sophie used the scissors to cut the finger or toe nails of the baby doll in a way which suggested she was anxious about being hurt or frightened. But in the last sessions, though she occasionally tugged at the baby's hair, she showed more concern, the kind of concern she felt that she herself needed. It was interesting that she used both the doctor kit and the more ordinary brush and nappies of parenting as if she were saying that the baby in her was still vulnerable and needed "doctoring" as well as looking after. While she was anxious about going home, she also let her father know that she thought he could help and care for her, although there were times when she also missed her mother. The father became increasingly interested in understanding Sophie's play, and she soon began speaking. There was more tenderness in his responses to her, and he showed more empathy towards what she was experiencing about the leaving.

Overall, the father was more aware of the negative aspects of his wife's poor parenting, and was more able to recognize and protect the children from these worrying aspects, while also recognizing the importance for them of continuing contact with her, provided that there were clear boundaries set up for the meetings. Initially, the mother tried hard to muddle these boundaries, and the father needed a lot of help to be able to manage them. But he was able to take a more realistic attitude to his wife's disturbance and put the children's needs first.

In the family sessions, the family were more cohesive, and the children were carrying less of the anger as the father was more able to acknowledge his own anger.

The father and children settled well into their home and were doing well a year later. The mother needed continuous support by her local mental health team.

Example three

Two parents become a couple

BACKGROUND

The C family consisted of mother, father, their four-year-old daughter Tanya, and a baby son, Simon, born during the first weeks of the family's admission to the Cassel. The family were referred by their solicitors because Tanya had been taken into care because of multiple admissions to various hospitals for no discoverable medical reason. Her mother had taken her on many occasions to the GP and to Accident and Emergency, claiming that she had stopped breathing and had had to have mouth-to-mouth resuscitation. Investigations led the social services to be concerned about the mother's relationship with her daughter, and a possible diagnosis of Munchausen's Syndrome by Proxy began to be considered. The girl was removed into foster care with an interim care order while investigations continued. In fact, by the time of the admission, father had been assessed to be safe with his daughter, and she was living with him, while the mother had to live with her own parents as she was not allowed to look after her daughter on a day-to-day basis. A considerable number of experts were called in to look at the situation. There was no clear agreement about diagnosis, but a general agreement that mother was a risk to the child, that she needed therapeutic input, and that her new pregnancy was a worry in that the new child would also be potentially at risk.

There were some aspects of the family that could fall within the range of so-called Munchausen's Syndrome by Proxy, or Factitious Illness Syndrome, such as the repeated hospital admissions for no discoverable physical cause, the mother's apparent need to have contact with doctors, and some disturbances in the mother–child relationship. Our own experience of assessing and treating families of this kind generally reveals more clear lying about the child's condition. For example, one mother caused a previous child to go into a coma by administrating salt; another put her own blood into the baby's nappy; while another gave aspirin and paracetamol to her child, which made her ill. The mothers are generally self-centred and like to control both their emotions and other people. They tend to have severe anxieties about their own bodies. There may be marital difficulties, which contribute to the presenting symptoms, as well as major disturbances in the mother–child relationship, which may be seen only after close observation. Although often saying the right things about their children, which may be convincing on the surface, they are in reality often emotionally cold and distant, with little capacity to empathize with their children. They may find it difficult playing spontaneously with their children, whom they see very often as mere extensions of themselves, to be used as they see fit. At times, the children are seen as objects to be used by their mother for mere comfort for themselves. The mothers who successfully completed the treatment programme revealed powerful and primitive aggressive fantasies, centred around their own bodies and their children. At times, they were near to collapse and disintegration, and needed considerable amounts of help and support. As will be seen, there were some aspects of the C family that corresponded to this kind of clinical picture, mainly with regard to the mother's difficulty with emotions, though there was less intentional harm to the child than one sees in those other families.

Initial interview

The couple presented as cooperative and willing to make an effort to be reunited as a family. Mother was articulate but anxious. She said that she recognized she had a problem and had been doing a lot of thinking since Tanya was removed into care. She thought she over-reacted when Tanya had difficulty breathing. She had watched the good foster parents deal with her when she held her breath, and now realized that her own reactions towards this were abnormal, because of her being too anxious. She now wanted help with this anxiety. When asked about where she though the anxiety came from, she thought it might be from her father. She recalled that she herself held her breath when a child, and her father could not deal with it, but just left the room, although her mother was better at it. There was also a history of some abuse, though not from the parents.

When asked about Tanya's frequent hospital visits, Mrs C said that she understood that she took her there so often because she then had the company of the staff. She described how lonely she felt if she were on her own with her anxieties. Since her daughter was born, she had the recurrent thought that Tanya was going to die soon. She became so afraid that she might overlook something that she took her to the doctor all the time.

Mr C was relatively uncommunicative, and gave only brief answers to questions. He was willing to support his wife, though was rather shocked at the prospect of help for himself, as he felt he had no difficulties as such. He found it difficult understanding why his wife was anxious all the time. He did admit that after Tanya's birth, when his wife was diagnosed with a post natal depression, he also felt low, but managed without medication. He also agreed that there might be links between his wife's problems and the fact that his own mother had had psychiatric problems when he was a child.

Tanya herself seemed well cared for, and there was a good and strong attachment between her and her parents, though clearly she had been affected by mother's constant anxieties. The father seemed protective towards her, but somewhat cut off from the effect on her of his wife's anxieties.

There was eventual agreement for a family admission, helped by joint funding from the local mental health services. The fact that professionals were in agreement about this admission, that there was no conflict at court about these proceedings, despite the anxieties aroused by the family, greatly helped to make the whole process of admission both relatively easy and therapeutic. One cannot emphasize enough how useful it is to have such professional cooperation around the court process. It is then possible to avoid the bitterness inevitably aroused by litigation, not to mention the high financial costs.

The assessment

As a result of our assessment we had a strong recommendation for the family to remain at the Cassel and to begin a period of intensive treatment, with a view to rehabilitation. We found that there was a significant risk to the new baby from the mother, if she were simply to return home, and that there was a difficult marital dynamic that had been going on for years and that had contributed to the difficulties with Tanya. However, the couple were also motivated for help and willing to engage with treatment. Overall, the feeling that the prognosis for change was reasonably good, given the fact that they had already begun to make changes in the assessment period. At first, the mother took the attitude that the professionals were making a fuss over nothing, but within a short time she realized what a lot she had to work on, around her relationship with both her children and with her husband.

It was decided that, because of the mother's problems, she would not be allowed initially to be alone with Tanya at any time. If the father was not around, the mother and Tanya would have to be in public places, and the family were not allowed to leave the hospital unaccompanied. In family interactions, not surprisingly, given the previous arrangements, mother saw herself as an outsider, while the father saw himself as the one who would fix everything. He came across initially as very compliant. He appeared to feel that if he did everything that was asked of him, he could not be blamed if things went wrong. While of course, in the end, he had not been the "ill" parent, there was a sense in which all problems were projected into the mother, leaving her with all the guilt.

The baby was born during this period, and there then ensued a difficult period for the family. The mother found the early days with the baby difficult because of feeding difficulties, and there was increasing tension between the couple. In addition, Tanya began to have increasing difficulties around food, becoming faddy and fussy and not wanting to eat her meals, particularly when both parents where together at the table.

The mother–baby relationship was initially rather fraught when the baby wanted to feed. In fact, the baby fed hungrily from bottles, while the mother was tense. The mother also often gave the baby water to settle her. The mother found it difficult enjoying these early experiences with the baby. Although there was also some warm interaction from both parents towards baby Simon, the mother's bonding with him was full of anxiety. Tensions between the couple also increased, so that they could not agree on when the baby needed feeding and whether or not to leave him to cry and for how long. Tanya's increasing demands on them only added to the tension. The couple showed rather a rigid response to the baby's needs. They could not empathically respond to him when he was hungry, so that they ended up at times keeping the baby waiting for a feed, with the result that he was desperately hungry. This seemed to correspond to the parents' own issues about how to deal with greediness and vulnerability in themselves

These kinds of issues with Simon were almost identical to those that arose when Tanya was a baby, when she was failing to thrive and needed repeated hospital admissions. The couple were able to acknowledge the parallels between their current conflicts and the past, and how the mother at that time was unable to cope with Tanya, particularly when she was left alone with her at the times her husband was at work.

With the child psychotherapist, Tanya was at first at ease with her father, but rather insecure with her mother and uncertain how to interact with her. The mother, who could be very articulate, found it difficult to provide physical comfort for Tanya. The father was secure with himself being the main carer, but did not encourage Tanya to interact with his wife. However, neither did the mother act as if to claim her daughter. When Tanya was seen with the mother on her own, she was very cautious. She was initially interested in a toy crocodile. In the first session, the crocodile came out of the box by accident and mother held it in her lap. Tanya reacted fearfully to this event, and subsequently she was a bit frightened by the crocodile. This seemed to represent her anxiety about what her mother would do.

Overall, the mother found it difficult to identify with her daughter, and difficult to express her feelings. She often left the therapist, and also Tanya, with a sense of disconnection between words and feelings, a problem which seemed fundamental to the mother's difficulties.

Not surprisingly, Tanya was preoccupied with the baby, both before and after he was born. She took on the role of the mother and wanted to look after the baby. The therapist wondered if perhaps Tanya was showing her concern about who was going to look after her in the new family situation.

Tanya was more confident and comfortable with her father. He would begin sessions by sitting on the floor and playing with her at her level. It was noticeable that in these sessions with the father, she could play with the same crocodile that had frightened her in her mother's presence without any concern. He himself, however, did wonder if he might have problems in setting boundaries for Tanya, compared with his wife, who was more able to do so. He was unsure about whether it would be better for Tanya if he were a parent who could keep clear boundaries, or whether it would be more fun for her to have someone who could allow her to do things that perhaps her mother would not allow her to do.

He described Tanya as being quite controlling when they were living together at home, "a bit like a wife". It felt that their closeness could be problematic at times and he felt as if Tanya had some sort of control over him. Tanya herself was a little confused about her father's role, and in one session she played with a crayon that she pretended was lipstick, and put this on her father's lips. Tanya showed interest in the doctor's set, and revealed that she had memories of when she was given Calpol through a syringe into her mouth when she was a small child. In one session with the father she showed how this happened, and he explained that that was the way that his wife would give Calpol. He felt he was completely removed from what was going on between Tanya and her mother. He described one time when Tanya was taken to hospital. When he came home, he saw Tanya as perfectly happy with her mother. He went to bed because he was working long hours, put ear plugs in his ears in order to sleep, and then found himself being woken up by his wife who told him that Tanya needed to be taken to hospital and that the ambulance was coming. This revealed his tendency to cut off from all sorts of conflicting and difficult feelings, particularly concerning his wife's risky behaviour.

In a session soon after the baby was born, Tanya was particularly anxious. She kept saying that she could not do things she could usually do, such as unscrew the top of a small bottle. She kept saying, "I can't, I can't". To this the father always responded reassuringly that she could do this, but could not really think why Tanya was having such feelings at that time. He often used reassurance that everything was fine, rather than face whatever feelings needed to be faced. This left Tanya often lost and insecure about having someone who could recognize what she felt.

Tanya used sessions with the therapist on her own very well, relieved to be able to use the space for herself, without having the burden of having to deal with either parent—her mother's anxiety and emotional distance, and her father's difficulty in listening to her own needs. One of the main themes in her play was about being dropped and things being dropped, no doubt related to her fear of being dropped by the parents, both in the past and in the present with the new baby around. Tanya also played a lot with the doctor's set, often using the toy syringe to put things in her mouth. She kept giving the therapist medication as if that was a way of letting the therapist know something of her experience.

In her adult psychotherapy sessions, Mrs C first of all said how fed-up she was about being depressed and on antidepressant medication, which was unhelpful (the latter was subsequently reduced and stopped). She felt a complete failure and was upset that Mr C was close to Tanya and about the fact that he believed it was entirely his wife's fault that they were at the Cassel.

Over the next sessions various issues emerged. Whether Tanya ate or not it seemed, in the mother's mind, that she was doing this for her parents. It was as if she could not think that Tanya would eat for herself. After the birth of the baby, the mother became increasingly preoccupied with abdominal and back pain. She spoke to the therapist like a chronic invalid. She seemed to find it easier to bring her physical pain to other's attention rather than her emotional pain. She blamed her pain on not being able to be active and playful with Tanya.

With regard to her husband, she found his reassurances irritating. She felt he did not allow her to have her own feelings. But she also admitted that she found it difficult knowing what Tanya felt. There were links between this difficulty and the relationship with her own mother, who was impenetrable. Mrs C was used to switching off in order to cope with unpleasant feelings.

In his therapy sessions, the father gradually began to use the opportunity to explore his feelings. Part of the legacy of his mother's own mental illness was of an overwhelming sense of responsibility, that it was up to him to cope and keep everything going, no matter what. He admitted being afraid that his wife would kill herself; the constant fear of loss made him in effect keep his distance as a form of protection. He managed intolerable feelings by cutting off, and this could make him appear to be controlling.

In the couple sessions, initially, the meetings seemed quite devoid of feeling. Both partners were exceedingly polite, both to the conjoint therapists and to each other. Then it became possible to start talking about how afraid they both were of each other's feelings, and of not being able to do the right thing. It was a relief for the husband to hear his wife say that all she wanted from him was to know what she felt and to listen; he wasn't expected to act. It seemed the first time that they were able to begin to know one another, though there was a long way to go before they could become a safer couple.

In the first family session, the father sat on the floor with Tanya, who used him as a chair; she only approached her mother when she asked Tanya to show her a toy that was similar to one they had. In the second session, after the birth of the baby, the mother sat on the floor with Tanya close to her. The parents had recently received our interim reports, and were taken aback by some of the comments. The father felt he had had a good report and the mother a bad one. She cried, saying that she did not know how to think about her feelings as she was so used to switching them off in order to cope. Tanya patted and hugged her mother in order to comfort her. When the baby became unsettled, Tanya began drawing on her own cheeks with felt tips, as though scratching herself. Neither Tanya nor the baby could be settled and the session had to be ended a few minutes early. One of the main themes of the family sessions became that of it being difficult to find a couple who could look after the children. One of the parents, usually the father, would remain like a child on the floor, playing nicely, but also not able to take a more adult parental role. Tanya would be left carrying the burden of trying to link the parents together into a couple.

Our recommendation for treatment was accepted by their local professional network, who managed to arrange joint health and social work funding to support the placement. They all felt that only intense work at the Cassel could possibly help the family to change, and similar facilities were unavailable locally. It was also felt that it would be wrong to split up the couple just because of the absence of such local facilities. The recommendation was accepted by the High Court judge involved in the case, and interim care orders continued to be in place until a final hearing some months later, with occasional direction hearings in place to hear about progress.

Subsequent progress

Three months later, treatment was progressing, although there was a considerable way to go because of the family's difficulties. Therapy consisted of a mixture of individual, couple, and fortnightly family sessions. Both parents seemed to be committed to the treatment process, although they revealed considerable difficulties as a couple. One of the main issues seemed to be how to help the family move from unhelpful means of communication such as denial, or medical illness, or psychosomatic complaints to more appropriate symbolic means, where feelings could be put into words. Tanya often spoke for the family because of these difficulties. It was also felt that her eating problems were an expression of the family's difficulties in taking things in.

In her individual therapy, the mother talked about having felt deprived and rejected all her life. She had to steal for the things she needed as a child. She dealt with her feelings of inadequacy by using food and by bullying. At home, as long as surface communication was reasonable, she could switch off unpleasant or worrying feelings. But she found Simon's occasional prolonged crying intolerable and got very tense. She displayed her frustration on a few occasions, once, for example, hitting a wall after a session so hard that her hand had to be checked at the local casualty department. She had an episode of breathing difficulties with pain in her arm and neck, and again had to be taken to hospital, where muscular pain was diagnosed. Her husband was unsympathetic to her, and she felt angry that people thought the pain was psychological in origin. When her baby had a period of pronged vomiting, staff worried that she might be poisoning him. When the therapist took this up as a possibility, the mother was incensed. She did not actually express her anger directly with the therapist, but was angry outside the session. The mother found it difficult to show any emotions spontaneously to the therapist; the therapist was seen as an all-powerful authority on whom the patient was dependent, but from whom she could not gain any satisfaction, except indirectly. Her relationship to her significant objects is one in which they mostly served to meet her needs. If there were a conflict or a difference, this was experienced unconsciously as being deprived or rejected. Consciously she felt inadequate and blamed. She had developed a delinquent way of trying to have her needs met via illness, both her own and her children's. However, this was unsatisfying as it made her dependent upon remote authority figures who could be critical and depriving. The husband was also cast in this role at times, and it was difficult for them both to extract themselves from this position. The result of that state of affairs was that the children's needs were overlooked.

In the father's individual therapy, work was done around his unexpressed feelings, such as his fear about getting angry in case his anger became destructive. In addition, he revealed quite a complex relationship with authority figures, whom he felt he had to appease and from whom he would keep issues secret. Indeed, in the couple sessions, both parents revealed their views about the staff as suspicious and authoritarian; yet they themselves were not fully open about what was happening. For example they did not reveal that Simon had been sick before he was due to go home one weekend, in case we prevented it. The father also failed to reveal his massive financial problems, which had been piling up without him dealing with them.

In these couple sessions, Mrs C often felt rejected by Mr C when he withdrew, and she was left feeling she was to blame for this. He began to acknowledge that he found her anger too dangerous to face, and that it was safer to withdraw. They both admitted that they had avoided being honest with one another for fear of the consequences. Mrs C feared that he would reject her and Mr C that she would be overwhelmed. Usually only one of them at any one time would be genuinely expressing a feeling, while the other was either confused, placating, or superior.

In the family sessions, the mother was more able to be worried and to express her anxiety about not knowing what to do. She mentioned her difficulties about not feeling close to Tanya, and that she feared closeness because she expected hurt and humiliation. The father remained emotionally removed in a number of these sessions, although this was increasingly challenged. Tanya could become quite disruptive in these sessions, for example by using the felt tips on her skin and face. This seemed to happen whenever there was a lot of unspoken tension or anxiety around. She was clearly carrying difficult feelings for the parents, a situation that needed to shift if she were to remain safe in the family.

Tanya continued to make good use of her own individual therapy. For some time she used her sessions in a non-verbal way, playing but not talking. At times it felt as if she were a baby who was trying to find a way of communicating something the therapist could not quite understand. She was often preoccupied with the baby doll. She became the mother who fed and changed the baby and made sure the baby was all right. At other times she was a mother who dropped the baby, who did not seem particularly concerned about the baby, who was left on the floor or somewhere in the room. Being dropped became a major theme, no doubt related to her baby brother's birth.

Tanya continued to be interested in the doctor's set. She still often put a syringe in the baby's mouth. She gradually revealed that what was being put into the baby was not nice. After verbalizing this for the first time, she regressed in the session and became a baby with a blanket around her, and also placed a corner in her mouth, as if she could not say any more.

At times, it was hard to have a sense of who Tanya really was. She tended to go from one toy to another, and it took time for her to settle and play with the intention of communication with, or involvement of, the therapist. In some of the sessions, she talked about the toy tortoise being trapped under the door, and in one session she trapped an ant under a plastic lid and told the therapist about the ant being trapped. So it seemed that Tanya felt trapped at times. Some of her feelings might get trapped and then it would become hard to understand her, and for her to understand herself and what she is really feeling. Because of this, she could present as a child to whom it was quite difficult to warm, and she found it hard to warm towards other people. This was matched by the therapist finding herself struggling to relate to Tanya, and having difficulty in finding words that would match Tanya's feelings.

Tanya was particularly upset in a session where she told the therapist that her mother had been taken to hospital (for some psychosomatic complaint). Tanya became withdrawn after this and eventually began to cry, saying that she was going to be sick, and then that she needed to go to the toilet. It was unusual for her to cry so much; it was the first time that she could show some of her real upset. Indeed, Tanya was a child who had to hold herself together, and usually found it hard to reveal how vulnerable she felt. This corresponded to the family's difficulty in funding a safe way to talk about their feelings.

Simon was a responsive baby. However, at first there were worrying features of the mother–baby relationship. There was little eye contact at first between Simon and his mother, and little time when he sat relaxed on his mother's knee. There was concern that he was given basic care but then quickly placed in his buggy, with little evidence of him being enjoyed as part of the family. When the child therapist focused on this with the mother, it became clear that she did not know how to just have her baby alongside her in close but not intense contact. She alternated between focusing on Simon very closely in a way that could be intrusive and disturbing to him, and almost forgetting him when in conversation with the therapist.

As the mother became aware of this situation, she became quite sad, recognizing that, unless she could develop a more close relationship with the baby then it would become increasingly hard for the baby to become really attached to her. This was the kind of problem she also had with Tanya. The therapist encouraged the mother to sit with Simon on her knee while they talked, checking in with the baby every so often, and also helped her to try to follow the baby's cues about what he wanted and what he was interested in, rather than just saying what was in her mind.

When the child therapist saw the couple together, they were also encouraged to read the baby's cues, and the father to support the mother in trying this. In fact, the baby responded well to the father, who knew intuitively how to relax with him. However, there were also times when he was cut off from the baby and could, for example, mechanically change the baby's nappy without any preparation, so that the baby was left rather stunned. It was at those times that he found giving attention to the baby overwhelming.

The conflicts between the couple could also get in the way of their working together to support each other with the children, so that it was easier at times to separate off into two pairs. However, there were also times when one could see them helping each other, and Tanya responded positively when they could do that.

Overall, we felt that we were in the early stages of a difficult yet worthwhile treatment process, and that we needed to continue this work as both parents were willing to commit themselves to it.

A few months later, progress had continued and rehabilitation plans were under way and accepted by the court. In this example, the court continued to have a useful monitoring role, a place where reports had to be lodged and examined without the added pressure of litigation.

The mother had made significant changes. She was more able to be open and honest about her feelings, and how self preoccupations could interfere with her ability to keep her children in mind. She acknowledged how her somatic symptoms could be used to mask her emotions. The father began to see how he avoided taking adult responsibility, and preferred to remain a child, able to play on the floor with his own children, but less able to function as a father and husband. The couple were able to see how they avoided relating to one another as adults, so that there were four children in the room in family meetings, each with their child needs waiting to be met. Tanya still felt she needed to get the parents together, although was relatively less anxious. She still had some eating difficulties; she could be resisting and challenging of her parents at mealtimes. Her eating had improved, but she still took only small amounts. The parents also needed a lot of encouragement to persist with her at these times rather than collude with her wish not to eat. In her own therapy sessions, Tanya began bringing a comfort blanket, which she used to deal with anger or sadness. However, its use gradually lessened over the months, as she became more able to express her anger without excessive anxiety. As discharge from the hospital approached, we set up a handover to local services, and helped arrange for ongoing therapeutic outpatient work, including individual therapy for the mother, to which she had to travel some distance. The family's rehabilitation seemed successful, and the family were doing well, more than a year after leaving the hospital.

Example four

Single mother and child, history of domestic violence

BACKGROUND

Miss D and her son, "Tim", aged six months, who was in short-term foster care, were referred by her solicitor to see whether or not she would be capable of using psychotherapeutic help at the Cassel in order to be rehabilitated with her son. Another expert, also instructed by her solicitor, had seen the family and had recommended the Cassel, though the local authority were against this and were recommending that he be adopted. The main objection to Miss D having treatment concerned her history of having been in a violent relationship with Tim's father on and off for some years. Their previous son had been removed and had been adopted because of this relationship, which had placed their child in a position of unacceptable risk. There was an attempt to rehabilitate the mother locally with her previous child, when she said that she had left the violent partner. However, it became clear that she had not separated from him and the domestic violence continued as before, with the mother often denying the reality of her bruises and offering inconsistent explanations for them. An independent expert found that her son had an anxious attachment to his mother, that he was in a situation of some risk, and that adoption would be best for him. Social services did not consider that there had been any change in the mother's circumstances or attitude with the prospect of the new baby, nor was there any change, in their view, after he was born. However, there was agreement that she be assessed again by an independent expert, and mother and son were placed together in a foster home for them both, where the mother did reasonably well with child care, so that her son was satisfactorily bonded to her. The worry, of course, was about her long-standing problems, and how these would affect her care of her son in the community without such intense support.

The new expert's assessment found that the father had a long history of alcohol abuse, as well as a long history of violence, including assaults on others, leading to imprisonment, as well as an intense and unstable relationship with Miss D. She herself could be diagnosed as having an emotionally unstable personality disorder of the borderline type. She had a long history of difficult relationships, involving family, schoolteachers, classmates, and boyfriends. She was impulsive, reported long-standing feelings of emptiness, periods of depression, and fear of abandonment, all consistent with such a diagnosis. She had a low tolerance of frustration, leading to frequent outbursts of temper, which, when combined with her long-standing feelings of loneliness, emptiness and fears of abandonment, could lead to a combination where there was a serious risk of the needs of the parent being put before the needs of the child, with neglect and also, in this case, being in the middle of violence between the partners a very real possibility. She had great problems with intimacy; there was little to suggest that any of her relationships had ever been free from violence. The expert considered that she would be at high risk of behaving violently towards her new child if given the sole responsibility for his care.

He considered that there was little prospect of the father being treatable, as he had no insight into his problems or any wish to change. With regard to the mother, there was some insight about her difficulties and their link with her past, including a history of being abused physically and sexually, and a wish to change her violent behaviour. However, the opinion was that out-patient therapeutic work in the community would stand little chance of being successful, given her long-standing pattern of difficult relationships, and that for that reason the Cassel should be considered as the only other feasible option.

Initial assessment

I did think it was worthwhile proceeding to a full residential assessment of mother and son, despite the worrying history. There were two main issues to be considered. First, mother had been Tim's main caretaker since his birth, and, although they were both in foster care together, with some limited supervision, she had in fact managed to look after him all that time. There was no major concern about the mother's day-to-day care of the baby. From my own observations, there was a clear bond between Tim and his mother. Indeed, she was still breast-feeding him.

It seemed to me not in his interests to remove him suddenly at that point without at least some attempt to look at rehabilitation. Second, however, the main stumbling block to rehabilitation was clearly the history, including the mother's recent involvement with a violent man, Tim's father. She did tell me in an interview that she had definitely left him that time. She had not seen him for four months, which was confirmed by the social worker. Thus, although one needed to retain a certain amount of scepticism about whether or not she had in fact left him for good, there were indications that she had a genuine wish to separate from him. In addition, she expressed to both me and the other expert a wish for therapeutic help, which she had not yet received and had declined in the past. She realized that unless she did something to sort herself out, she would continue to run the risk of becoming involved with unsuitable men.

In my interview, mother and son were brought by the social worker.

I first saw mother and son and then invited the social worker to come in later. Mother looked after Tim well during the interview. He was a bright, alert boy, then eight months old and developmentally normal. He was interested in toys that he was offered. He sat up on his own and played quite well from time to time. He consistently had eye contact with his mother. She seemed able to keep him in mind throughout the interview. It was obviously difficult talking to me and also looking after him, but she managed to do so. For example, at one point while he was sitting up and playing, he started to fall over, but mother caught him in time. On another occasion he started to whinge, and mother offered him some juice, which he took well and which comforted him. At the end of the interview, with the social worker present, he began to be particularly fraught, and with some encouragement the mother gave him a brief breast-feed to calm him down and also to prepare him for the journey back.

She described the current foster arrangements, which included a certain amount of supervision, although she was left alone at night, and she was left to look after him for a significant part of the day. She wanted a chance to look after him permanently, although social services wanted Tim to be adopted. She also wanted psychiatric help for herself, such as counselling. She had asked for help. Interestingly, it was at that moment in the interview that Tim started falling over and she caught him; as if he was communicating something about his mother, or both of them, needing to be held and caught as it were.

Overall, her care of Tim in my presence was good. His attachment to her appeared normal, and he was developing well.

My impression from direct questioning was that she had separated from her violent partner, but that without appropriate help she would drift back to him or to someone similar. He had been controlling and was a drinker, and had prevented her from having friends as he was so jealous. She was violent to him as well as being the recipient of his violence. There were links between her violent relationships and the fact that her father had been violent to her mother, which she accepted as possible. She had also been sexually abused by a family member from puberty and for some years; this remained a secret. She had had a turbulent adolescence, and turned to drugs and alcohol to blot out feelings of emptiness and low self-esteem connected with both her deprived upbringing and her sexual abuse.

Although the mother's history of violent relationships was worrying, there was a good bond between her and the baby. It seemed difficult to contemplate removing the baby from her care at that time, particularly as she was clearly expressing a wish for help. At the very least it seemed clear to me, and to the other expert, that there should at least be a thorough assessment of her capacity to change. In some ways, she was showing features of post traumatic stress disorder, in which there can be a kind of freezing of emotion and a shock-like clinical picture. One often sees this in women who have just left violent men; they often take quite a time to recover from their experience. It was also my experience that a good relationship between parent and child, as shown in this case, has is own positive prognostic significance. If a mother is able to make such a relationship with a dependent being, then it does show some capacity to relate to a child. The ability to deal with dependency is fundamental in assessing significant change.

Social services' view was that it was still not in Tim's interest to pursue such an assessment. They were worried about the effect of a positive assessment; that there would be a risk that if we were to pursue rehabilitation it would be even more difficult to remove the child if things broke down later. This is a commonly used argument against pursuing assessments for rehabilitation. But it is obvious that one can never predict exactly what will happen to the family during treatment. All one can do is to make a reasonable prediction once all the clinical evidence is available after the initial assessment phase. One can look at factors in favour of rehabilitation and those against, and weigh them all up in order to make a recommendation. Then, the longer one goes on with rehabilitation, the more likely is the chance of success. With this mother, the main factor against her even proceeding to an assessment was clearly the history of violence, and the doubt about the truthfulness of her having separated from her partner. The fact that she was in a supportive foster home, though useful for the care of the baby, was also somewhat unreal, in that she protected from the temptation of seeing the violent partner. On the other hand, it gave her the time and space to stand back and ask for help.

Social services still opposed the assessment, so, as is often the case, I had to appear in court to justify my opinion. I was cross-examined at some length, but maintained my view that the positive factors outweighed the negative factors, and that it would be both unjust to remove the child from his mother and not in his interests.

While I could not guarantee a successful outcome—I was not a prophet—I considered the chances of recommending rehabilitation were reasonably good, provided the mother could engage with the therapeutic process. In these situations, one can view therapy as a vital tool in the assessment process, not something to be considered apart form the rest of the assessment. In the event, there was agreement for the assessment to go ahead, helped by the fact that the Guardian was strongly in favour of the assessment, and that the NHS were prepared to fund the mother, so that social services just had to fund the baby. Social services continued to support the assessment and subsequent successful rehabilitation of the family, including various difficult times, which made the whole process both more easily manageable than is unfortunately often the case and more rewarding to all parties.

Initial assessment

At the initial assessment meeting, we had further evidence of the mother's good care of her baby. In the sessions with the child therapist, Tim showed himself to be lively and adventurous, interested in toys and in exploring his environment. The mother seemed to enjoy this robust side of him. She encouraged him to pull himself up and try to stand, but at his own pace, and she was relaxed about minor falls and bumps, helping him to take them in his stride and recover quickly. Tim was very attached to his mother, and the therapist saw some warm and tender contact between them. He was also sensitive to her state of mind. Thus, in one session she arrived having scalded her hand. She was in pain, although she minimized this; but it was striking to see that Tim bumped himself more than in any other session, and then tipped himself backwards, as if showing how his mother's accident had thrown him off balance.

Mother talked about her difficulty in helping Tim settle and stay in his cot. The therapist thought that in fact the mother saw this as a staff difficulty rather than hers. She enjoyed having him in her bed, as the closeness and comfort was important to her. Also he was still being breast-fed, and they both fell asleep during the night-time feed. The mother added that sometimes Tim bit her then. There was thus an issue about how the mother was going to manage greater separation as Tim got older, while also maintaining appropriate closeness.

The mother was vulnerable to feeling lonely. When the child therapist saw them on the day they were admitted, mother was unhappy, feeling that she had been torn away from her foster family. Later, she appeared more confident and assertive, but it seemed that she would turn to Tim for comfort when feeling vulnerable. The mother, however, found it difficult to explore this kind of issue; she would easily become defensive, feeling criticized or blamed.

Mother attended her individual therapy punctually, taking care to make appropriate baby-sitting arrangements for Tim well in advance (unlike a number of other parents on the Unit). At their first meeting, she filled the time recounting her history and explained to the therapist that she had come to the hospital in order to work on her being at risk of returning to a violent relationship. She assured the therapist that she had not seen her partner for some months. The therapist's initial impression was of someone eager to please, someone keen on telling the therapist all the right things. At the same time, the therapist took up how Miss D was taking pleasure in not succumbing to the temptation to see her ex-partner, and this animated Miss D, helping her to *look* at the possibility of making better relationships. She was also able to express grief about losing her previous son, and remorse about what she was not able to provide for him.

The mother also brought an angry side to the sessions, and talked more openly about her violent feelings, including giving details of the violence between her and men. She could hold on to destructive grievances. What then became clearer was the difficulty she had in experiencing loss, and how she feared being overwhelmed by depression. The latter was experienced as an enemy that had to be fought on all fronts. Internally, she tried to combat feeling low with excitement, with a physical kind of high, an adrenaline rush. She was able to admit that aggression and violence could deliver such an antidepressant rush. It did not matter whether the violence was in her or whether she was confronted with it in someone else. Externally, she fought with those who threatened to inflict on her feelings she could not bear. She would engage others in this battle, if she felt too weak to win it by herself.

Subsequent progress

Separation became the central theme of her work in her therapy. She began to trust her therapist as someone there to help her. For a while, she was able to look at the difficulties in her relationship with Tim. She saw how worried she could be about not getting things right for him, and how she could cut off from this worry altogether when it threatened to overwhelm her. She was also able to reveal her guilt about her previous son, whom she abandoned in pursuit of her partner.

However, with the impending arrival of the Christmas break from the therapist, Miss D began to become involved with another, male, patient, trying to get him to leave his partner, repeating a pattern in her life. This seemed related to what happened after her own parents had broken up, when she became very special to her mother and cared for her. She was allowed to sleep in her mother's bed when she herself was frightened. But then a step-father moved in and she was pushed out of the bed, and left frightened on her own.

Miss D was still struggling with feelings that were either too painful to bear, such as loneliness, betrayal and guilt, or too destructive to face, such as anger and vengefulness. Her need to cut herself off from feelings altogether, as well as her particular difficulties over loss and separation, must have had some impact on her relationship with Tim, although she also continued to engage with treatment.

In sessions with the child therapist and mother together, he showed signs of developing normally and of being a lively boy, walking and beginning to talk, and playing with good concentration. However, mother was resistant to weaning him from the breast (at fifteen months at this point) and disliked talking about this issue. She still gave him the breast at night, so that when he went to bed and also when he woke at night, the mother used the breast to settle him. She found it hard to believe that there could be a satisfying alternative way of comforting him. The feeds also seemed to help her feel connected, at which time it was difficult for her to differentiate what felt important for her from what was best for him. Her needs for intimacy and comfort, as well as feeling important and indispensable, were being met in this way. However, by maintaining the close relationship through feeding, she was also keeping at bay more hostile feelings that could emerge between them, if they were really able to face Tim's task of individuation. Nursing staff noticed that when they were not physically close, mother could appear to forget him. If she was preoccupied with other things, she appeared to find it hard to follow him, and then he would fall and hurt himself. Then he made his way back to her for comfort. It seemed to be the case that she found it hard to help him move away from her, while supporting him in her mind as he did so. The lesson for Tim was that it was dangerous to become independent, and that the way to keep in touch with mother was to be hurt or upset.

Thus, her own difficulties around separation and individuation were clearly being transmitted to her son. None the less, progress was possible, as the rehabilitation process got under way, with her leaving foster care and moving into her own home. Despite some stormy periods, the mother gradually became more able to tolerate in herself sad feelings of loss and regret. Instead of turning to anger and vengefulness when faced by depressive feelings, she became more in touch with her vulnerability. This was revealed, for example, when a patient she had made friends with came to the end of her treatment, and a nurse she was also fond of left. The emotional good-byes, as well as her own sense of having moved on, put her in touch with her impending discharge, and how much she was now more aware of appreciating relationships.

The relationship with Tim improved, particularly after she finally gave up breast-feeding him. He became more lively and explorative, more robust, confident, and determined.

He was more separate from his mother, although there was still a warm attachment and loving interactions between them. Not surprisingly, the issue of setting limits for him soon came up, as he became more independent and also had some tantrums. This coincided with a phase of her feeling more depressed, as she became more in touch with issues such as separation and the loss of her previous son. One of the main focuses of work then became how she could protect Tim from her own distress.

Soon after this, and as discharge loomed larger, Miss D began to regress to previous modes of behaviour, which is, of course, typical of any termination phase. She was aggressive, often getting into rows, particularly with staff. This was clearly related to her feelings of abandonment as rehabilitation was well under way. These feelings made her panic about her ability to manage on her own, and then she became angry about being left in such a state. She then became furious with the very people whose help she feared she could not do without, setting up a vicious circle from which she found it almost impossible to break out. She became less aware of the impact of her state of mind on Tim, who reacted by being more anxious, particularly at night, when he would wake up wanting to go to her bed for comfort.

There was a strong link in her mind between loss and guilt. A sense of loss and abandonment immediately brought to mind her previous son whom she abandoned and lost. Only, in this scenario she was not the victim but the perpetrator. This seemed to be the really unbearable part of what the prospect of leaving with Tim had stirred up. At some level, she knew that unless she managed to come to terms with her own guilt about she did, she would not be able to live comfortably with Tim.

Despite these concerns, by the end of treatment, there was a warm and loving, but not over close relationship between mother and son. More work was done in her therapy about how she used excitement, through sex and violence, to ward off the underlying issues about loss and separation. Further outpatient therapy was recommended to continue this work. Mother and son continued to do well in their community, and the care order was removed some two years after discharge.

Concluding remarks

As illustrated in the above examples, rehabilitation of disturbed families can be time-consuming and anxiety-provoking, even when the work proves to be ultimately successful. One can never afford to take one's eye off the ball, as it were. Just as things seem to be going well, it is possible that a new issue will arise and cause concern. But then, that is part and parcel of the work. Provided that the child care continues to be good enough, that the child is kept safe and the attachment between parent and child remains reasonably secure, the work towards rehabilitation can continue. There are bound to be rocky periods; indeed, it would be strange and worrying if there were not, as the parents need to bring their difficulties out into the open for them to be dealt with. It can also take time to get to the heart of the parents' problems, as shown, for example, with Miss D, whose issues about separation and individuation were underlying her manifest problems around violence.

Stopping the rehabilitation process may occasionally need to happen when the risks to the child become too great. This may happen if the parent becomes consistently unable to remain focused on the child, who may then be unduly suffering. If this happens, it usually does so in the early or preliminary stages of rehabilitation, when the parent may suddenly find the prospect of having ultimate responsibility for their child just too daunting. Also, once the fight for rehabilitation is over, once the "enemy" in the form of the authorities has been removed, then the parent may find it too difficult having no such effective place as these authorities to receive their projections. The child may then become the target for the projections, which can make the work towards uniting parent and child impossible, even with a considerable amount of therapeutic help. Again, if this is to occur, it usually does so in the preliminary stages of the rehabilitation process.

Removal of children from their families at these times is difficult for all involved, even when it is obvious that it should occur. For the parent it is, of course, excruciating, though the main initial response is often just that of anger and blame towards the professionals, rather than remorse about their own role in the breakdown of the placement. Such a reaction, though understandable, also reflects the difficulties around recognizing their own contribution, which led to the decision to remove their child. For the professional, these times are difficult because of the disappointment about the lack of progress and the end of hope for the rehabilitation. For the child, there may be relief at being no longer burdened by their parent's projections and other inappropriate feelings, but of course there will also be disappointment and loss, depending on their age at removal. Ongoing therapeutic work may be necessary for the members of the family, but they may be quite unmanageable at that time because of the anger and bitterness they feel about the removal. However, the child may be desperate for a chance to talk to a professional about what happened. Offering at least a few sessions with a child therapist at this time may be very helpful to the child and their future mental health and well-being, reducing the feeling, which inevitably they have, that they were responsible for the breakdown of the placement.

In two of the above examples there was a considerable amount of legal litigation, which added a burden to the rehabilitation process. In the last two examples, once the court agreed to the outcome of the initial assessment, the social services and health resources agreed to the whole treatment package, which of course greatly reduced disruption to the treatment of those families. At the same time, it must be said that it is often thanks to courts and to the motivation of both parents and their lawyers, that families who otherwise would have been written off as hopeless can have a chance to be rehabilitated. The courts remain, at times, the last hope for a family of remaining together, the last bastion of the child's right to family life with their parents.

CHAPTER SIX

Conclusions

The many examples given throughout the text have, I hope, demonstrated that the issues concerned with making decisions about a child's future in a disturbed or conflict-ridden family situation are often highly complex and emotionally charged. Time and again one has to face the fact that there are no perfect solutions in this field. Each situation requires a thorough assessment and a good deal of discussion to resolve issues, either just before going into court or in meetings planned prior to court. Unfortunately, the nature of the conflicts in the family often mean that professionals are left trying to pick up the pieces, as it were, rather than attempting to put the family together again.

Sometimes, it feels as if a bomb has hit a family, producing such fragmentation and disruption that all one can do is to try to find a place where the children are no longer in acute danger. However, it can be distressing to come across situations where there has been no attempt to address the family's problems at the first crisis situation, when the "bomb" first hit them. For example, I recently saw a mother of four children who had had an acute depressive breakdown some three years previously. This had occurred after she was beaten up by her new partner. The beating brought up early memories of her childhood abuse. These overwhelmed her to such an extent that she quickly de-compensated and became acutely depressed, at one point threatening to kill the children. The latter were accommodated with a relative while the mother was admitted to a psychiatric ward where she received antidepressant medication.

The problem was that, though she recovered from the acute crisis, she was left feeling vulnerable, with constant flashbacks of her past abuse. These symptoms were never tackled, nor was she given counselling or therapy. She found herself unable to look after her children, who became increasingly disturbed. There were also concerns that she might harm the children, because of her previous threats when she was acutely depressed. The children were eventually accommodated in various places, without a core assessment being undertaken. The situation drifted on for two years without any clarity, by which time the children were in great need of therapeutic help. By that time, there was no question of the mother being able to look after them all again, though she did wish to have a chance with one of them, the most disturbed, and she also wished to have therapeutic help for herself, which was unavailable where she lived.

This unfortunate situation clearly revealed breaches in good practice; but it reflected not only an unforgivable lack of foresight and planning, but also the dearth of effective resources common to many parts of the country. When local authorities cannot fill their social service vacancies, it is hardly surprising that such services are often stretched beyond their limits, leaving the families without appropriate help. The courts may eventually be used as a place where effective planning can be put in train, but, as with the family above, this may be just too late to do anything except clear up the mess left by the breakdown of both the family and the local service.

The limits of the legal system to address children's needs are well described in detail in the book *Children's Welfare and the Law*, by King and Trowell (1992). For example, they suggested that much could be done to improve the quality of justice for those children and parents who become immersed in court proceedings, suggestions which by and large have still to be followed. They recommended (King and Trowell, 1992, p. 106) the improvement of court facilities, some lessening of the ordeal-like nature of the hearings, and the education of the legal profession in basic principles of child-care and development. While there has been an extensive programme of education for the lawyers, there has been little improvement of the facilities in many parts of the country, including the High Court. Nor has the atmosphere in court changed; it remains adversarial. While the best judges show a remarkable degree of fairness, wisdom, and knowledge of the issues, there remain those who think they are in a criminal court, that the complexities of family life can be dealt with by some sort of short, sharp shock. In any event, however kind the judge, the problems inherent in using the court to deal with children's welfare and their placement remain.

Place of psychoanalysis/impact of trauma on the child

Psychoanalysts, with their theories of child development and their experience of the effect of childhood trauma both on the children themselves and on their subsequent development, have been in the forefront of trying to provide guidelines for making child placement decisions. Several key elements in making clinical judgements for children were provided by Anna Freud and her collaborators—Goldstein and Solnit—in their classic book, *Beyond the Best Interests of the Child* (1973), based firmly on psychoanalytic principles. Their three main guidelines have become axiomatic. These are:

- that placement decisions should safeguard the child's need for *continuity of relationships*.
- that these decisions should reflect the child's, not the adult's, *sense of time*.
- that the decisions should take into account the *limits* of the law to affect interpersonal relationships.

Continuity of relationships implies that children should suffer the minimum disruption to their ongoing relationships. Thus, multiple placements are undesirable, with long-standing traumatic effects on the child. Brief placements, for example with a short-term foster parent, may be necessary but should be accompanied by clear long-term plans, where possible, and appropriate ongoing contact with the absent parent.

Appreciating the child's sense of time implies the need to take account of timescales in the child's life, and the avoidance of unnecessary delay in making decisions about placements.

> The significance of parental absences depends upon their duration, frequency and the developmental period during which they occur. The younger the child, the shorter is the interval before a leave-taking will be experienced as a permanent loss accompanied by feelings of helplessness and profound deprivation. Since a child's sense of time is directly related to his capacity to cope with breaches in continuity, it becomes a factor in determining if, when, and with what urgency the law should act. [Goldstein, Freud, & Solnit, 1973, p. 42]

The timescale of the child may or may not match that of the parents' capacity to change in their relationship to the child. A delicate balance often has to be drawn between giving the parents a chance to prove they can look after their child and the effect delay may have on the child's capacity to make lasting attachments. Additional "reality" factors to consider are the following: that courts are over-booked, and so hearings may take place months down the line, thus adding to delay and uncertainty; that finding and preparing suitable long-term carers takes time in itself; and that there are occasions when alternative carers are abusive, adding to the children's trauma. Such factors should not be an excuse for delay, but they certainly add to the complexity inherent in making decisions about a placement.

Such complexity only confirms the third point about the limitations of the law to supervise interpersonal relationships, and the difficulty in making long-term predictions about the outcome of a legal decision. Thus:

> No-one—and psychoanalysis creates no exception—can forecast just what experiences, what events, what changes a child, or for that matter his adult custodian, will actually encounter. Nor can anyone predict in detail how the unfolding development of a child and his family will be reflected in the long run in the child's personality and character formation. Thus the law will not act in the child's interests but merely add to the uncertainties if it tries to do the impossible—guess the future and impose on the custodian special

conditions for the child's care. [Goldstein, Freud, & Solnit, pp. 51–52]

This point has already been emphasized in dealing with, for example, issues around contact, where it is inadvisable to impose rigid conditions for a considerable length of time, as people and situations may change. Of course, research into the long-term effects of child placement decisions may help to reduce some of the uncertainty about what is the best course of action; but it can never remove the burden of knowing what to do for the best in a particular case.

Anna Freud and her collaborators also emphasized that, while the child's interests were paramount, this principle should take second place to the one that placements should provide the least detrimental available alternative for safeguarding the child's growth and development. This standard incorporates the three guidelines. The least detrimental alternative is:

> . . . that specific placement and procedure for placement which maximizes, in accord with the child's sense of time and on the basis of short-term predictions given the limitations of knowledge, his or her opportunity for being wanted and for maintaining on a continuous basis a relationship with at least one adult who is or will become his psychological parent. [Goldstein, Freud, & Solnit, 1973, p. 53]

The advantage of adopting the least detrimental principle is that the phrase immediately conveys to the decision-maker that the child is already traumatized by his environmental circumstances, that he or she is greatly at risk; that decisions need to be made speedily to prevent further damage; and that the adult's best interests do not trump those of the child. However, I would prefer to retain the principle of the child's best interests as primary, as it has a more positive emphasis, even accepting the reality that the best worst option is usually all that can be achieved.

Other principles involved in making decisions about children include the need to provide a thorough assessment of the family. But in order to do so effectively, one has to deal with, or recognize, anxiety, both the family's anxiety and that of the professional network. It is important to attempt to make emotional contact with often deprived and suspicious parents, who may initially spurn such attempts, particularly when they feel persecuted by the local authority for having removed their children. Making and using good observations of the family's functioning, both during an assessment interview and at contact visits, is essential in order to provide clinical evidence for one's expert opinion.

Assessment of the parents' personalities is described in detail in the chapter on assessment. There, I emphasized the usefulness of an expert having psychotherapeutic skills in assessing the attributes and qualities that form part of the general character or personality of the parents.

In fact, the involvement of psychoanalysis and the law has a long history with regard to assessing the criminal personality, including issues of intention and degrees of responsibility that may also be relevant in the child-care field. Ferenczi and Abraham both worked for the courts in order to earn extra income to support their analytic work. Freud, who did little if any such work, did write a paper in 1906 on psychoanalysis and the establishment of the facts in legal proceedings (Freud, 1906c). This concerned how one can look at the reliability of a witness and try to establish the guilt of a criminal. Freud compared the task of the therapist to that of the examining magistrate. The therapist has to uncover the hidden psychical material, and, in order to do this, he will use a number of detective devices.

One of the main difficulties for the expert is to find a language that the court can understand, but that does not dilute the expert opinion. Freud provided a good model of how to make psychoanalytic ideas comprehensible to the court in his essay "The question of lay analysis" (1926e). The purpose of this work was to support Theodor Reik, a prominent non-medical member of the Vienna Psycho-analytical Society, who had been charged with "quackery". It is interesting that early in the essay Freud emphasizes the power and magic of words in the analytic treatment. One could add that the court is also a place where words are given almost magical status at times. There have been occasions when I have been cross-examined on the precise meaning of one particular word, which for me represented just a passing comment.

One example of how a passing comment can become enshrined in legal language concerned *Re: M (Residential Assessment Directions)*

[1998] 2 FLR 371. Mr Justice Holman heard this case, in which I gave evidence. It concerned a single mother with a personality disorder and her young child, who was in interim care. When the issue of whether or not it was worthwhile to pursue an assessment of mother and child, I was asked to give an estimate of the chances of success. I replied with a shrug that it was perhaps 50/50. I really only meant that I was not that certain about the outcome, but thought it worthwhile to proceed at least to an assessment, after which I would be clearer about the prognosis.

From that point, one of the key elements at court indicating the need for a family assessment became whether or not the chances of success were at least 50/50. While I am gratified, not to mention, flattered, by this use of my passing phrase, produced while under the immense strain of being on the stand for some hours, it has made me a little wary about the way that lawyers' use of words can be very precise, in a field where complexity is the order of the day. Perhaps that is why words are so important in court; they can give the impression that we all know what we are doing, when quite often we are struggling with uncertainty.

To return to Freud's contributions to the law once more, of particular interest is his description (Freud, 1916d) of those criminals who commit a crime in order to get relief from an oppressive feeling of guilt, the so-called "criminals from a sense of guilt". That is, guilt in some circumstances does not arise from crime but rather crime arises from guilt. One can see something equivalent with those deprived parents who cannot bear to feel guilt. They may go so far as to attack their children when the children remind them of their own unbearable feelings of vulnerability. Therapeutic work with such parents entails trying to get to the underlying or repressed guilt.

Melanie Klein (1927) developed Freud's thesis in her work with children. For her the criminal does not lack a conscience, but rather has too cruel a conscience, an unmodified super-ego, which operates differently from the normal and drives him to crime by pressure of guilt and fear. She writes

> One of the great problems about criminals, which has always made
> them incomprehensible to the rest of the world, is their lack of
> natural human good feelings; but this lack is only apparent. When
> in analysis one reaches the deepest conflicts from which hate and

anxiety spring, one also finds there the love as well. Love is not absent in the criminal, but it is hidden and buried. [Klein, 1934, p. 260]

While the situations in family law are somewhat different, in that there is not often a direct issue of criminal guilt, one is often dealing with a similar area, where the parent may have caused injuries to a child or placed them at risk (for which they sometimes do indeed have to face a criminal charge), and where the degree of remorse, owning up to responsibility, the quality of the guilt and the amount of anxiety available at assessment may well determine the outcome for the child. In addition, one may well have to work hard to uncover buried feelings of love and concern. The difficult issue, however, is knowing when it is worthwhile giving the parent a chance to uncover such feelings, and when the time it takes to find them matches the timescales for the child.

Other psychoanalytic thought particularly relevant in the family court includes Bowlby's attachment theory and its recent development through direct mother–child research; and Winnicott's many ideas about the nature of mother–child interactions as well as his work on delinquency and the antisocial tendency.

Examining the kind of attachment patterns that exist between parents and children has become basic to family assessments, as described in Chapter Two. When parents and children reveal good enough attachment patterns, the parents usually have a good recall of their childhood. They can also usually remember at least one good relationship in their childhood. The parents can respond sensitively to their children and are attuned to their needs. The children are secure and can deal with stresses and strains. But insecure patterns of attachment, such as avoidant, re-enacting, or disorganized patterns, predispose to, or are accompanied by, problems in parenting, with the parents unable to be attuned to their children in various ways, leading to a variety of problems with the children themselves. There is evidence (Egeland, 1988) that those parents who had been abused as children, and yet who had at least one good relationship, could overcome their abuse and not abuse their own children. Psychotherapy during childhood or adolescence could be one such good relationship, confirming the hope that providing psychotherapy to the vulnerable parent might have a protective function. Research at the Cassel (Fonagy *et al.*, 1996) has certainly indicated that those parents who can develop in therapy a capacity for self reflection can overcome the effects of their past abuse.

Bowlby revealed the link between emotional deprivation in childhood and subsequent disturbed behaviour, such as delinquency. Behind his thought were the ideas of Freud on the nature of object loss as described in "Mourning and melancholia", and Klein's observations on children, with their concept of the depressive position, and the various disturbances in emotional life resulting from failures to negotiate this position. Bowlby added empirical findings from his work with children deprived of their parents' ongoing care; for example, during the war and in hospitals. The presence of emotional deprivation remains, unfortunately, an only too common feature of many of the families who encounter the legal system.

Winnicott's ideas about the nature of the environmental provision necessary for a "good enough" parent–child relationship are also fundamental in this field. It is now taken for granted that in the earliest phase of life, one is dealing with a special state of the mother, which he called "primary maternal preoccupation" (Winnicott, 1958a, p. 301) when the mother becomes acutely sensitive to the baby's needs and the baby is provided with an intense caring and dependent relationship. Without this special state of mind, a normal attachment may not develop.

Winnicott also emphasized how what he called the "antisocial tendency", can be linked to failures in emotional provision. With the antisocial tendency, there is a loss of something good that has been experienced, but has then been withdrawn. The withdrawal "has extended over a period of time longer than that over which the hold can keep the memory of the experience alive," (Winnicott, 1958b, p. 309). For Winnicott, there is a way in which various kinds of antisocial behaviour, such as stealing and lying, can be seen as a sign of hope for the child, as they are at least trying to search for an environmental provision that has been lost and which they need, even if this is in a form that is socially unacceptable. He describes how the nuisance value of an antisocial child is an essential feature, and also at its best a favourable one, indicating a potential for recovery of lost capacities.

One could extend such understanding to many of the families who come into contact with the courts. The latter may represent for them all kinds of parental figures, but can also come to represent the whole of their depriving and failing environment, even more so as the court has the power to remove their children, sometimes the parents' only source of goodness, however much in reality they have neglected them.

Unfortunately, with some parents it is difficult to discover any positive environmental provision in their past; it is then not so much an issue of the withdrawal of something positive but of little positive being provided in the first place, and thus little identification with a caring figure. Such parents may literally have to be taught how to parent their child. Winnicott (1958c, pp. 222–223) also describes how the young child can deal with environmental disturbances such as the mother's absence when there is active adaptation to the child's needs. The child can then be in a state of undisturbed isolation. In this state, he can make a spontaneous movement and the environment is discovered without any loss of the sense of self. There is a respect for process, a sense of continuity, one experience will follow another; when something occurs in the environment, there is an appropriate reaction. The child can build up memories of a mother who is both actively present and returns when absent, and who can thus *hold* a situation over time.

But when there has been a failure of good enough adaptation, with environmental impingement, the child returns to a state of restless isolation. The absence produces no return, or there is such a long wait for the return that there is a loss of the sense of self, and the child is in a state of solitary and anxious waiting.

Such early experiences can help to understand the psychic situation in adults. The neurotic can stand absence without loss of the sense of self. The borderline goes in and out of states of unthinkable anxiety, but there is still some sense of a return of the mother.

But with the psychotic, there is no return, and a sense of utter desolation and emptiness. The absence of the maternal image takes possession of the mind.

Those children who have experienced major disruptions in the early holding environment, as one so often sees in the families who come to court, may retreat later from the reality of the social world into a private time, or into a state of almost psychotic timelessness, where comings and goings are irrelevant. With some traumatized and often abused adults there are also pathological states in which lived time is avoided by a whirlwind of activity, and they may experience rapid changes between extremes in their mental state. The whirlwind of confusion, with so many comings and goings that it is impossible to register any coherent pattern, may be both a defence against experiencing chaos and a way of re-creating an excited mental state, egged on or precipitated by drug use or sexual excitement. They may need the whirlwind in order to feel alive, for they have not had the sense of time kept going by the mother.

One can see a variety of disorganized attachments with those children who have been subjected not just to emotional detachment but also to physical and/or sexual abuse. My own experience of working with such children and their families at the Cassel Hospital (Kennedy, 1997a) reveals that these children are often haunted by their abuse and unable, without considerable help, to free themselves from its consequences. They often cannot concentrate on a task for long, as if there has been a massive disruption in their capacity to link experiences over time. They appear over-stimulated, with poor impulse control, and they may have a haunted, driven quality to their relating, and a tendency to be aggressive and testing of boundaries. Sometimes they may show inappropriate sexual behaviour; they may go in and out of confusional states when they become very anxious, particularly about being abandoned, and they have great difficulty in trusting adults. The parent–child relationships are usually pathological, with varying degrees of disorganized attachment patterns. There is often role reversal, in which the child tries to control the parents' comings and goings, while the parents have problems in maintaining ordinary child–adult boundaries. These parents often have difficulty in being emotionally attached to their children, with inhibition of the capacity to play. In the child, and probably also in the parent, there is a loss of, or failure to develop, the capacity to use meaningful symbols; so that, as it were, no symbolic interchange is possible. The parents are often inconsistent, at times cut off and self-absorbed. The children themselves seem to make a particular kind of powerful emotional impact on their parents and other caretakers, as if they are desperately trying to get the parents to acknowledge their needs, while also attacking them for having failed them. Many of these children have had to suffer in solitude, and have had to bear, on their own, horrific experiences.

My own experience of the psychoanalysis of the abused adult is that such a person will re-create the emotionally absent parent at some point. This is the parent who could not bear the child's pain and vulnerability, and who has left the child with a sense that the environment has fundamentally failed them, and that there is a kind of breach, or unbearable gap, in the parenting experience. An unbridgeable gap may suddenly appear between patient and analyst, which either party may be tempted to deal with by some kind of precipitous action, such as termination. Bearing unbearable emotional pain is an issue in any analysis, but with the abused adult it becomes acutely relevant.

Evidence of impact of mental illness on children

A number of the families who come into contact with the courts have at least one member of the family with a mental illness. There is considerable evidence for the impact of mental illness on children's development and their own mental health. This includes Rutter's work in the 1960s, which highlighted the risks to children's development of having parents with a psychiatric disorder, as well as more recent work, such as for example, that of Lynne Murray on the clear effect on the child's emotional and cognitive development of having a mother with post natal depression (Murray & Cooper, 1997). Several aspects of children's development can be affected by their parents' mental illness, including their physical, cognitive, social, emotional, and behavioural development. Quality of parenting and family interaction affected by the parent's illness are the key factors here. There is also the vast literature on the importance of understanding early attachments, and how the nature of these attachments is related to subsequent mental health in adults and children.

Finally, there is the accumulated clinical experience of working with individual children and adults as well as the whole family, which reveals the many, complex, and sometimes subtle, effects that disorders in the adult may have on their children, either directly or through various indirect means. These may be direct general effects—such as creating a burden for the child, and making them feel unduly responsible for their parent, as well as having to endure the stigma of mental illness.

More subtle general effects can be seen in the various kinds of unconscious intergenerational forms of communication that can be seen in families. For example, one may ask how the suicide of a grandparent affects subsequent generations. There will be the direct traumatic effect on those who are left, but then the subsequent, more complex effect on family relationships across generations. Such forms of communication are most commonly seen in the children and grandchildren of Holocaust survivors.

Enid Balint has also shown how elements of the subject's pre-history can be unconsciously communicated across generations. She showed how certain experiences of one of her adult psychoanalytic patients were related to the patient's mother's traumatic history of being abandoned as a baby, and how this was unconsciously communicated to the patient. Balint demonstrated how there are times when a set of experiences is unconsciously communicated to the child as an alien formation, a piece of the mother's experiences that have not been metabolized. The child then has these experiences by proxy, as it were; but as they do not belong to them, they are not connected to the rest of their experiences, and they may then form a nucleus of symptoms which becomes like a foreign body inside the personality.

> This foreign body may have to remain in place until it can be dealt with by its "host" when he or she is strong enough to do what the original recipient of the trauma could not do. Such a chain of events means that one generation has to resolve traumata that another generation has failed to. [Balint, 1993, pp. 117–118]

One may ask in this context how our continuing failure to attend to the effects of mental illness on children will affect future generations, who will have to pay for this neglect. More specific effects refer first of all to how the parent's mental illness can affect their parenting capacities. Typical patterns with the mentally ill parent include one or more of the following:

1. The *psychically absent parent*. The parent may be good enough when well, but cannot focus adequately on the child when ill,

for example during a period of acute depression. The child experiences a parent who comes and goes psychically, but at least has a notion of a good parent, particularly if the other parent is supportive. The effect on the child's development will depend upon not only the capacity of the other parent, if there is one, to provide alternative care, or any alternative caring structure, but also on the age of the child. Murray's (1997) work clearly shows evidence that babies are significantly affected by their mother being severely depressed. This also clearly has implications for the kind of service provision that needs to be available to families.

2.   The *confused parent*. Having a deluded and hallucinated parent obviously can be very anxiety-provoking for a child, depending on their age and how they understand what is happening to their parent. Children of such parents may have to deal with their parent going in and out of hospital for treatment, or at any rate going in and out of confusional states. Without a reliable alternative carer or caring arrangement, and/or community support, such children may suffer from significant emotional harm.

3.   The *unreliable parent*. Typical situations here are with the addictive parent, whose drinking or drug abuse repeatedly puts their children at risk. Domestic violence, often associated with alcohol abuse, may also be a feature of the family, exposing the children to direct attacks on themselves, or to seeing their parent being attacked.

4.   The *unempathic parent*. This refers to those parents who are unable to be in touch emotionally with their children in major ways, thus exposing their children to a variety of risks, emotional, physical, or sexual. There is direct evidence that disordered attachments between parents and children are associated with an increased risk of family violence.

This is obvious really, in that if a parent is emotionally out of touch with their child, then their child is more at risk of being harmed in some way being severely neglected or abused.

5.   The *enmeshed parent*. These are parents who are unable to see themselves as separate from their children. They may be satisfactory parents of young babies, but when the child begins to show signs of independence, the parent may resent this and

find it difficult to encourage the child's growing need to explore. Similar problems may persist well into adolescence, with parent and child caught up in a confused system, where identities are merged and the adolescent cannot become independent of the family.

Any mental illness in a parent can produce one or more of these kinds of parenting problems. Those with personality disorders tend to be more associated with being unreliable or unempathic parents.

The future

In so many of the families described in the various examples given, the authority of the law has stepped in to take over the loss of the parent's own authority. Helping people to regain their authority as parents under these circumstances can be difficult, though it is possible, as has been described in Chapter Five. Parents have every right to go to law when they can in order to seek redress for what they feel are injustices.

However, these families not infrequently find themselves repeating with the authorities their own way of relating with each other. The authorities may then come to represent the family's own unsatisfactory parents, which may then make the family themselves feel constantly humiliated, punished, or misunderstood by those around them. They may then in turn attack and punish those whom they see as responsible for unnecessary persecution. It can be difficult for both the family and the workers around the family to extricate themselves from this kind of unhelpful dynamic.

This situation reflects the way that the child-care system is organized in England, with an adversarial legal system underpinning the way that social workers have to deal with deprived children. The fact that health and social services are usually organized separately, with their own budgets, only exacerbates an already conflictual system.

Other European countries organize themselves differently, and some deal with the parents of deprived children in more satisfactory and less conflictual ways. For example, in France and Germany it is taken more for granted that services for these families should be provided. The courts are clearly helpful and facilitating towards the parents, and removal of children is rare and a last resort (see Baistow & Hetherington, 1998, Baistow & Wilford, 2000, and Hetherington, Baistow, Katz, Mesie, & Trowell, 2002). In a comparison of cooperation between community mental health services for mentally ill parents and those for child protection in ten different European states and in Australia (Hetherington & Baistow, 2001), showed how poorly resourced England was, and how poor were services in general compared to other states. The English groups of workers talked more about lack of resources than any other group except Greece. The worst shortage was lack of professional time. The English workers were very pessimistic about change, and this was connected to their lack of resources, but also to the crisis orientation of the structures within which they worked, and to the fragmentation and the dominant non-interventionist approach. Other countries tended to intervene much earlier in difficult situations, before a major crisis erupted, which then of course would drain resources.

In France, the parents have a much more personal relationship to the children's judge, who has the power to order appropriate services but not the immediate power to remove a child. Hence the whole atmosphere at court is non-adversarial, and the court aims to find what is best for the child and the family. This way of organizing the court reflects French society's attitude to family and kinship structures, with emphasis on trying to keep children within the extended family structure, and also reflects the continental legal system, which is based on the quest for the truth.

While it is unrealistic to think that English law is going to change its whole basis overnight, the European dimension is already making substantial changes to the way that English courts approach legal arguments. The right of children to family life under the European Convention for the Protection of Human Rights and Fundamental Freedoms 1950, has already had an impact on the way that the English courts think about how to deal with problem families. But there is a long way to go before the Human Rights Act enables the English way of dealing with problem children and difficult families to change from being crisis led to an approach that takes for granted early and effective intervention and appropriate treatment.

REFERENCES

Baistow, K., & Hetherington, R. (1998). Parents' experiences of child welfare interventions: an Anglo-French comparison, *Children and Society, 12*: 113–124.

Baistow, K., & Wilford, G. (2000). Helping parents, protecting children: ideas from Germany. *Children and Society, 14*: 343–354.

Baker, A. (1995). What constitutes reasonable contact? In: P. Reder & C. Lucey (Eds.), *Assessment of Parenting* (pp. 247–261). London: Routledge.

Balint, E. (1993). *Before I was I.* J. Mitchell & M. Parsons (Eds.). London: Free Association Books.

Bateman, A., & Fonagy, P. (2001). Treatment of borderline personality disorder with psychoanalytically oriented partial hospitalization: an 18-month follow-up. *American Journal of Psychiatry, 158*: 36–42.

Bentovim, A. (1992). *Trauma Organized Systems.* London: Karnac.

Black, D., Harris-Hendricks, J., & Wolkind, S. (1998). *Child Psychiatry and the Law* (3rd edn). London: Gaskell.

Chiesa, M., & Fonagy, P. (2000). Cassel personality disorder study. Methodology and treatment effects. *British Journal of Psychiatry, 176*: 485–491.

Cooper, A., Freund, V., Grevot, A., Hetherington, A., & Pitts, J. (1992). *The Social Work Role in Child Protection: an Anglo-French Comparison.*

London: Centre for Comparative Social Work Studies, Brunel University.

Department of Health (2000). *Framework for the Assessment of Children in Need and their Families,* London: HMSO.

Diagnostic and Statistical Manual of Mental Disorders (DSM IV) (1994). 4th edn. Washington, DC: American Psychiatric Association.

Egeland, B. (1988). Breaking the cycle of abuse. In: K. Browne, C. Davies, & P. Stratton (Eds.), *Early Predictions of Child Abuse.* Chichester: Wiley.

Fonagy, P., Steele, H., Kennedy, R., Leigh, T., Matson, G., Target, M., Steele, M., & Higgitt, A. (1996). The relation of attachment status, psychiatric classification, and response to psychotherapy. *Journal of Consulting and Clinical Psychology,* 64(1): 22–31.

Freud, S. (1906c). Psycho-analysis and the establishment of the facts in clinical proceedings. *S.E.,* 9: 99–114.

Freud, S. (1916d). Some character-types met with in psycho-analytic work. *S.E., 14,* 310–333.

Freud, S. (1926e). The question of lay analysis. *S.E.,* 20: 183–258.

Goldstein, J., Freud, A., & Solnit, A. (1973). *Beyond the Best Interests of the Child.* New York: Free Press.

Graham, P. (2000). Treatment interventions and findings from research: bridging the chasm in child psychiatry. *British Journal of Psychiatry, 176:* 414–418.

Hetherington, R., & Baistow, K. (2001). Supporting families with a mentally ill parent: European perspectives on interagency cooperation. *Child Abuse Review,* 10: 351–365.

Hetherington, R., Baistow, K., Katz, I., Mesie, J., & Trowell, J. (2002). *The Welfare of Children with Mentally Ill Parents.* Chichester: Wiley.

International Classification of Diseases (2003). 10th edn. Geneva: World Health Organization.

Kennedy, R., (1987). The work of the day. In: R. Kennedy, A. Hayman, & L. Tischler (Eds.), *The Family as In-Patient* (pp. 27–48). London: Free Association Books.

Kennedy, R. (1997a). *Child Abuse, Psychotherapy and the Law.* London: Free Association Books.

Kennedy, R. (1997b). Assessment of parenting. In: N. Wall, (Ed.), *Rooted Sorrows* (pp. 73–84). Bristol: Family Law.

King, M., & Trowell, J. (1992). *Children's Welfare and the Law.* London: Sage.

Klein, M. (1927). Criminal tendencies in normal children. In: *Love, Guilt and Reparation and Other Works* (pp. 170–185), 1981. London: Hogarth Press and the Institute of Psycho-analysis.

Klein, M. (1934). On criminality. In: *Love, Guilt and Reparation and Other Works* (pp. 258–261), 1981. London: Hogarth Press and Institute of Psycho-analysis.

Murray, L., & Cooper, P. J. (1997). The role of infant and maternal factors in postpartum depression, mother–infant interactions and infant outcome. In: L. Murray & P. J.Cooper (Eds.), *Postpartum Depression and Child Development* (pp. 201–220). New York: Guilford Press.

Sturge, C., & Glaser, D. (2000). Contact issues. *Family Law, 30*: 615–629.

Thorpe, M. (1993). The assessment of personality. *Family Law, 23*: 293–296.

Thorpe, M. (1994). Personality assessment. *Family Law, 24*: 257–260.

Wall, N. (Ed.) (1999). *Contact Between Children and Violent Partners.* London: Lord Chancellor's Office.

Wall, N. (2000). *Expert Witnesses in Children Act Cases.* Bristol: Family Law.

Wall, N. (2002). Expert evidence 10 years after the implementation of the Children Act, 1989. Where are we? In: M. Thorpe & C. Cowton (Eds.), *Delight and Dole. The Children Act 10 years on* (pp. 75–90). Bristol: Family Law.

Williams, D., & Garner, J. (2002). The case against "the evidence"; a different perspective on evidence-based medicine. *British Journal of Psychiatry, 180*: 8–12.

Winnicott, D. W. (1958a). Primary maternal preoccupation. In: *Through Paediatrics to Psychoanalysis: Collected Papers* (pp. 300–305). London: Hogarth

Winnicott, D. W. 1958b). The antisocial tendency. In: *Through Paediatrics to Psychoanalysis: Collected Papers* (pp. 306–315). London: Hogarth.

Winnicott, D. W. (1958c). Psychoses and child care. In: *Through Paediatrics to Psychoanalysis: Collected Papers* (pp. 219–228). London: Hogarth.

INDEX